Science Panorama 6

Biology

Series Editors
Meenakshi Atal
Manjuli Mukherjee

Collins

Science Panorama 6

Biology

Series Editors

Meenakshi Atal

Manjuli Mukherjee

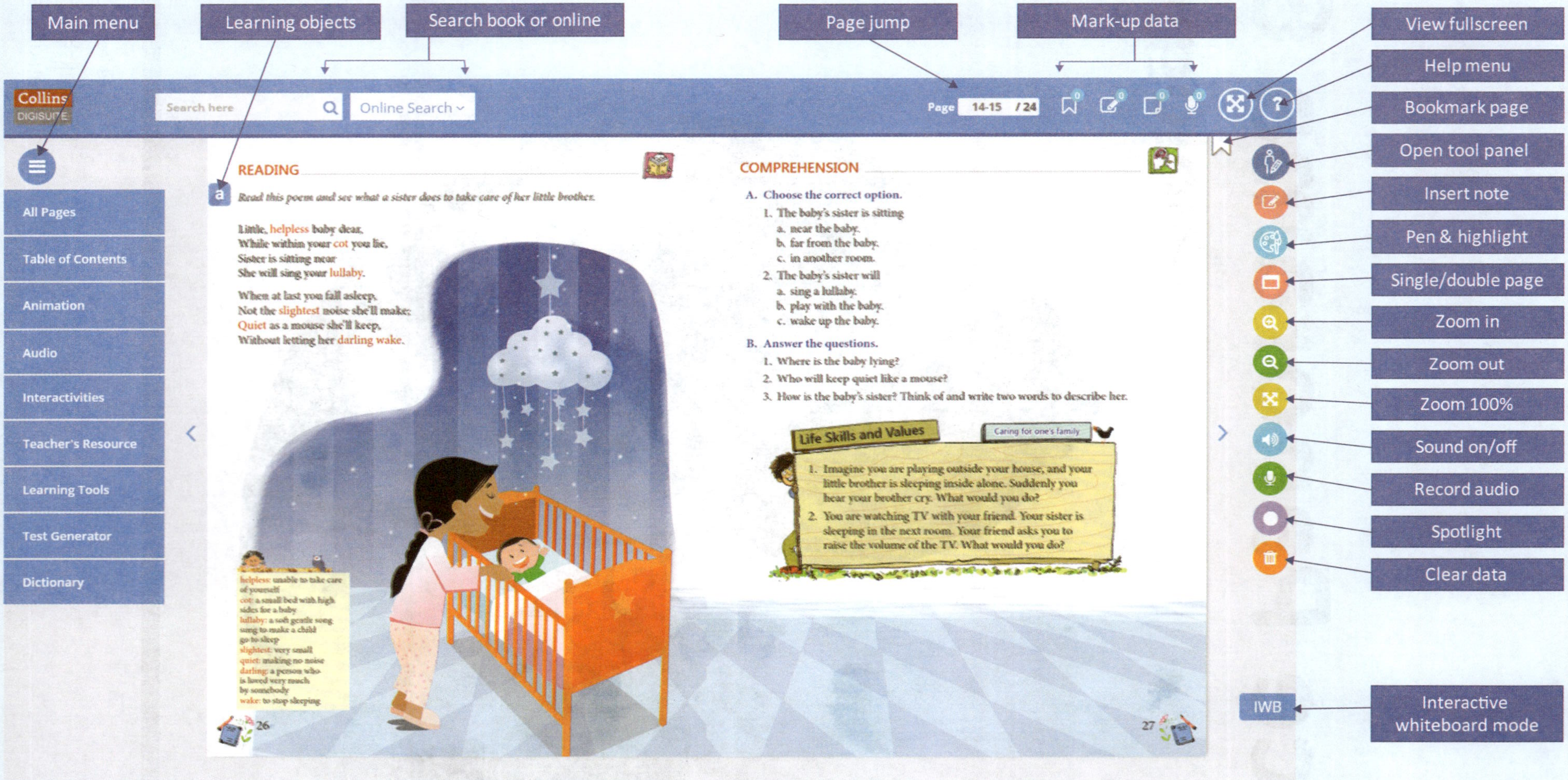

Student + Teacher		Teacher-only	
a animations	ia activities	lp lesson plans	tn teacher's notes
ilt instructor-led tutorials	w worksheets	w worksheets	ak answer keys
g games	v videos		
audio			

Preface

Science Panorama is a series of books for Classes 1 to 8, which includes 3 books each for Physics, Chemistry and Biology for middle school. The middle school series has been updated based on the **new syllabus** prescribed by the **Council for the Indian School Certificate Examinations**. In line with the new syllabus, a thematic, coherent and structured approach has been followed and all the new topics suggested in the syllabus have been included. Chapter-wise worksheets have also been provided to effectively integrate subject knowledge and life skills for overall development.

This updated edition also emphasizes on developing scientific skills such as observation, investigation, analysis, research and other inferential skills. It focuses on development of concepts as well as their application in real life. Sufficient examples from everyday life have been provided to help learners understand the concepts using age-appropriate language. Colourful illustrations and well-labelled diagrams have been included to engage learners and aid their understanding.

Some Key Features

Science in Context: Additional information on the topic being taught

Do You Know? Interesting facts related to the given topic

Greenathon: Some tips to keep the environment clean and green

Challenge Yourself: Questions testing students' ability to reason and extrapolate

Activities: Individual/collaborative activities to hone experimental and deduction skills

Know the Scientist: Famous scientists and their contribution to the topic at hand

Revision Zone: In-text questions for assessing progress in the course of learning

Keywords: Important words from the chapter along with their definitions

In a Nutshell: Summary of the chapter content

Mind Map: Flowchart for quick recapitulation

Exercise: Variety of questions given at the end of each chapter

Subject Integration Worksheets: To effectively integrate knowledge across subjects

Life Skills Worksheets: To create awareness, empathy and a positive attitude towards self and others

Assessment papers: Two assessment papers at the end of the book for effective evaluation

We would like to take this opportunity to thank all the teachers who reviewed the books and provided their valuable feedback. Special thanks to Ms Ela Kapadia, an educationist with several years of experience in teaching and curriculum development, for giving her suggestions, which helped in improving the quality of the content.

Any suggestions or constructive criticism from the users are welcome. We shall try to incorporate those in the future editions.

Authors

Key Features

Do You Know?

Interesting facts related to the given topic

> **Do You Know?**
>
> Earth is estimated to be around 4.5 billion years old. The first life form is estimated to have appeared around 3.7 billion years ago.

Science in Context

Additional information on the topic being taught

> **Science in Context**
>
> Some people have only 28 teeth. The remaining 4 teeth appear later during the age 17-21 and are called **wisdom teeth**. Some people do not have wisdom teeth at all!

Challenge Yourself

Questions testing students' ability to reason and extrapolate

> **Challenge Yourself**
>
> You have studied in Class 4 about microorganisms called viruses. They have not been included in any kingdom. Find out why.

Know the Scientist

Famous scientists and their contribution to the topic at hand

> **Know the Scientist**
>
> The concept of an energy pyramid was developed by **Charles Sutherland Elton** (1900-1991). He published this in his book *Animal Ecology*. These pyramids, therefore,

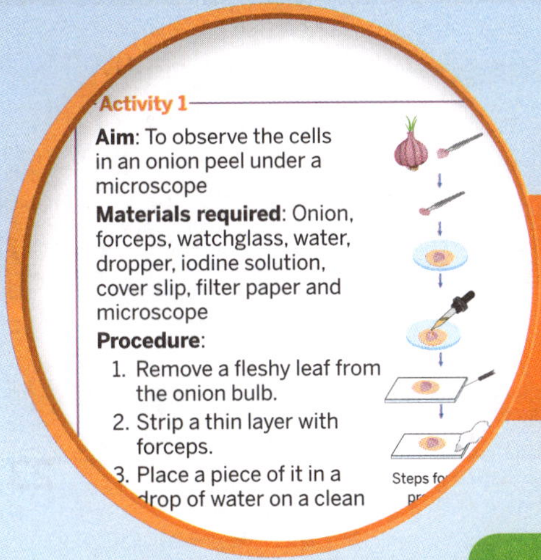

Activity

Activities to hone experimental skills

Revision Zone

In-text questions for assessing progress

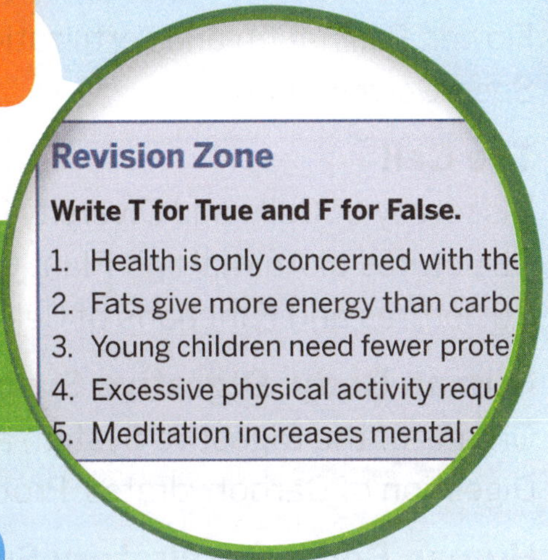

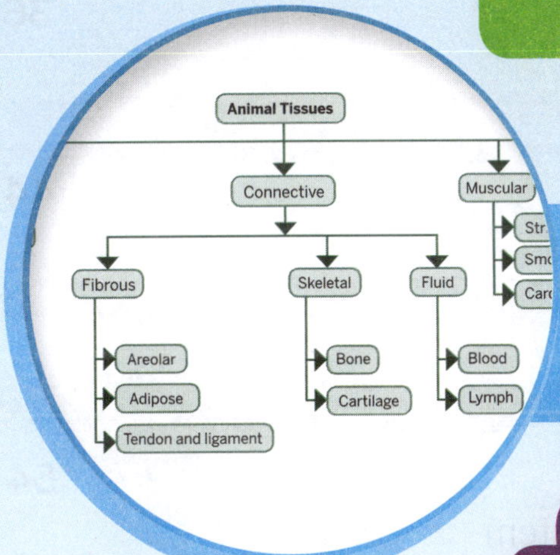

Mind Map

Flowchart for quick recapitulation

Exercise

Variety of questions given at the end of each chapter

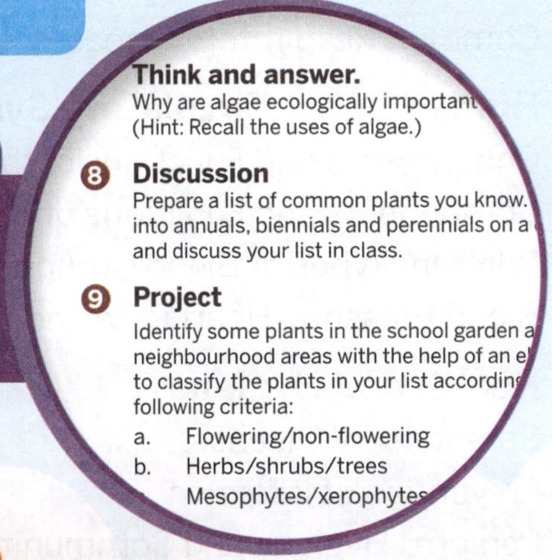

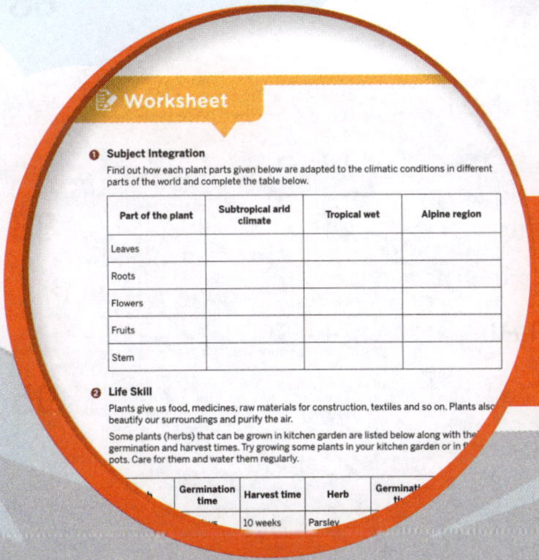

Worksheet

Thematic worksheets on integration of knowledge across subjects and Life Skills

Contents

Plant Life

1

What I shall learn

- Leaf and leaf modifications
- Flower
  - o Pollination
  - o Fertilization
  - o Seed germination

Introduction

There are more than 352,000 species of flowering plants on Earth. They are found in almost all the habitats. All flowering plants have a basic structure that can be divided into two main systems: root system and shoot system.

Leaf and flower are part of the shoot system. Now, let us look at them in detail.

The Leaf

A leaf is a thin flattened part of a plant that appears from the nodes of the stem and branches of a plant. The green colour of the leaves is because of the presence of the pigment called **chlorophyll**. Leaves are of different shapes and sizes.

▲ Fig. 1.1 Parts of a leaf

A typical leaf has a petiole, lamina and veins. A leaf is attached to the stem or branch with a stalk called **petiole**. The broad, expanded flat part of the leaf that is generally green in colour is called the leaf blade or **lamina**. Thin, clear lines on the lamina of a leaf are called **veins**. **Midrib** is the main vein that branches out to form smaller veins. Veins help in the transportation of food and water in leaves and also support the leaf structure.

Venation

The arrangement of veins in a leaf is known as **venation**. Leaf venation is basically of two types.

(a) Reticulate venation

(b) Parallel venation

▲ Fig. 1.2 Types of leaf venation

Reticulate venation: Arrangement of veins in a net-like pattern on both sides of the midrib is known as reticulate venation. This forms a complete network of veins. Leaves of hibiscus and red gram have reticulate venation.

Parallel venation: The leaf has a central, prominent midrib that gives lateral veins, which are parallel to each other towards the margin of the leaf. Parallel-running veins are often connected at intervals by short links. Leaves of banana and wheat have parallel venation.

(a) Simple leaf (b) Compound leaf

▲ Fig. 1.3 Types of leaves

Types of Leaves

Leaves can be grouped into two types based on the division of the leaf blade or lamina.

Simple leaf: Leaves with undivided lamina are called simple leaves. Examples include mango and maple leaf.

Compound leaf: Leaves in which the lamina is divided into several parts on a common stalk are called compound leaves. Examples include rose and neem leaf.

Activity 1

Aim: To identify the venation in different leaves

Materials required: Plain white sheets, pencils and five different types of leaves

Procedure:

1. Keep a leaf under a sheet.
2. Trace the leaf by shading with the pencil on the white sheet so that the leaf structure appears prominently.
3. Repeat the same for all the leaves on different sheets.
4. Observe the types of venation in each leaf you have shaded.

Observation:

- Leaf 1: ______________.
- Leaf 2: ______________.
- Leaf 3: ______________.
- Leaf 4: ______________.
- Leaf 5: ______________.

Conclusion: Some leaves have reticulate venation and some have parallel venation.

(a) Alternate

Arrangement of Leaves

The arrangement of leaves on a stem is one of the main factors that helps in absorbing sunlight for photosynthesis. The arrangement of leaves also helps us to classify the plants. There are three types of leaf arrangements.

- **Alternate**: In this type of leaf arrangement, only one leaf is present in the node and successive leaves appear at opposite directions. Examples include leaves of sunflower and china rose plant.

(b) Whorled

(c) Opposite

▲ Fig. 1.4 Arrangements of leaves

- **Whorled**: In this type of leaf arrangement, more than two leaves arise at a node. This makes it look like the leaves surround the node. Examples include leaves of Michigan lily and oleander.
- **Opposite**: In this type of arrangement, on a single node,

two leaves are present making it a pair. The pair of leaves is placed at right angles from each other making them appear opposite to each other. Examples include leaves of neem and guava.

Functions of a Leaf

- **Photosynthesis**: It is a process by which plants synthesize their own food using carbon dioxide and water in the presence of the green pigment chlorophyll and sunlight.

$$\text{Carbon dioxide + water} \xrightarrow[\text{Sunlight}]{\text{Chlorophyll}} \text{Glucose + oxygen + water}$$

- **Gaseous exchange**: Leaves have specialized structures for gaseous exchange. These are called **stomata** (singular: stoma). A stoma is a minute pore or opening with two bean-shaped structures called **guard cells** on either side of the pore. Stomata are usually found on the underside of leaves.
- **Transpiration**: It is the process of removal of water from the plant. Excess water in the plants is removed through the stomata.

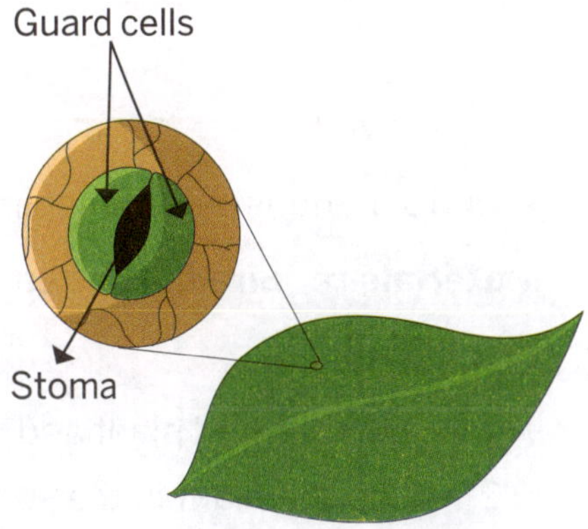

▲ Fig. 1.5 Specialized structure in a leaf

Activity 2

Aim: To show that photosynthesis takes place in leaves

Materials required: Potted plant, black paper, water, beaker, burner, test tube, spirit, water bath, forceps, glass slide, iodine solution, dropper

Procedure:

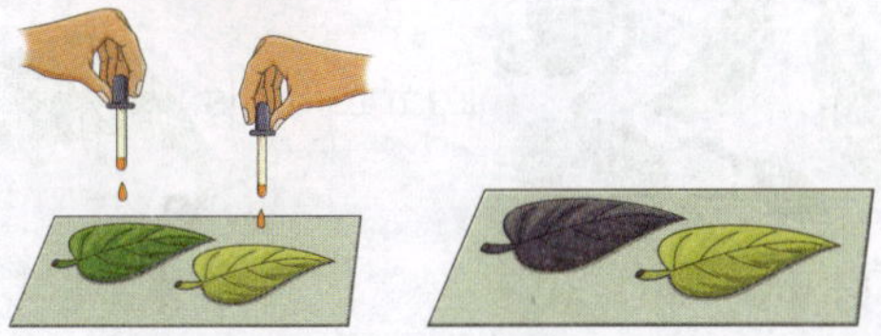

- Select a potted plant with broad leaves and keep it in dark for 24 hours before using it for this experiment. Take it out and clip a black paper over one of the broad leaves (name it A) of the plant and keep it in sunlight for half a day or a few hours.
- Then pluck out this leaf along with another leaf (name it B) from the same plant (to use as a control).
- Take about 25 mℓ of water in a 50 mℓ beaker and boil it using a burner.
- Remove the black paper from leaf A.
- Dip both the leaves A and B into the boiling water with the help of forceps for about 2 minutes (to stop all the metabolic functions of the leaves and to make them porous).
- Place both these leaves in a test tube and pour spirit to completely immerse the leaves.
- Keep the test tube in a water bath (beaker with half-filled water).

- Heat the set-up using a burner till the leaves turn white.
- Take out the leaves carefully using forceps and wash them with cold water.
- Place them on a glass slide and pour some iodine solution over both the leaves using a dropper.

Observation:

- Leaf B, which was exposed to sunlight, shows a blue–black colour all through the leaf, while leaf A, covered with the black paper, does not show blue–black colour.

Conclusion: Photosynthesis takes place in leaves and food is stored in the form of starch.

Activity 3

Aim: To demonstrate transpiration in plants

Materials required: A potted plant, some water, a polythene bag and thread

Procedure:

1. Take a potted plant and water it.
2. Keep the plant in the sunlight and cover it with a polythene bag. Secure the bag with a thread.
3. Observe it after some time.

Observation: The polythene bag near the aerial part of the plant shows tiny droplets of water on the inside surface.

Conclusion: Water vapour has escaped from stomata of the leaves due to transpiration.

Leaf Modifications

Leaves adapt themselves to different environmental conditions to perform special functions for their survival.

Modified leaves perform several specialized functions such as:

Support: Climbers like pea and grapevine have tender and weak stems. Their leaves get modified into thin, coiled structures called **tendrils**.

Tendrils provide support for the plants to anchor. Whenever they come in contact with a neighbouring object, they coil around it and help the plant to climb.

Leaf tendrils

▲ Fig. 1.6 Leaf tendril – pea plant

▲ Fig. 1.7 Leaf tendril – glory lily

Protection: Leaves of plants like cactus modify and develop into pointed structures called **spines** for protection. Spines in place of the leaves also help to reduce loss of water in the desert plants.

▲ Fig. 1.8 Cactus with leaf spines

Storage and protection of bud: Some leaves are modified to form scale leaves, which can store food and water. For example, in onion, the scale leaves protect the terminal bud, and also store food and water.

▲ Fig. 1.9 Onion – food storing scale leaves

Trapping insects: In insectivorous plants, leaves are modified to trap insects that sit on them. Plants are brightly coloured and attract insects.

- **Pitcher plant**: The tip of the leaf gives rise to a tendril that ends with a pitcher-shaped structure. The pitcher contains liquid and waxy slippery walls that help trap insects.

▲ Fig. 1.10 Pitcher plant

- **Venus flytrap**: In this plant, the leaves are modified into a trap. Leaves have two parts called **lobes** held together by a midrib. The lobes have fine hair and produce sap. There are spikes at the periphery of the lobes.

  The insect, attracted due to the sap, enters the trap and hence, disturbs the hair in the lobe. This triggers the lobes to close, leading to the entrapment and further digestion of the insect.

▲ Fig. 1.11 Venus flytrap

- **Bladderwort**: These plants have bladder-like structures that trap insects. These bladders are modified leaves having small openings with hair. The hair is triggered if an insect is at the opening. Then, the insect gets sucked into the bladder and digested.

Revision Zone

Fill in the blanks.

1. Leaves arise at the ________ (internodes/nodes).
2. A typical leaf is attached to the stem with a stalk called ________ (petiole/midrib).
3. In a banana leaf, the type of venation is ________ (parallel/reticulate).
4. In a compound leaf, the leaf has divided ________ (lamina/veins).
5. If there are more than two leaves at a node, it is called ________ (whorled/opposite).

Vegetative propagation in leaf: *Bryophyllum*

A type of reproduction where new plants grow from the vegetative parts of the parent plant, such as root, stem or leaf is called **vegetative propogation**. In nature, most plants reproduce vegetatively with the help of stems, roots or leaves.

Plants like *Bryophyllum* produce buds from the margin of the leaves. These buds drop off from the leaves and fix themselves to the ground and later grow into new plants.

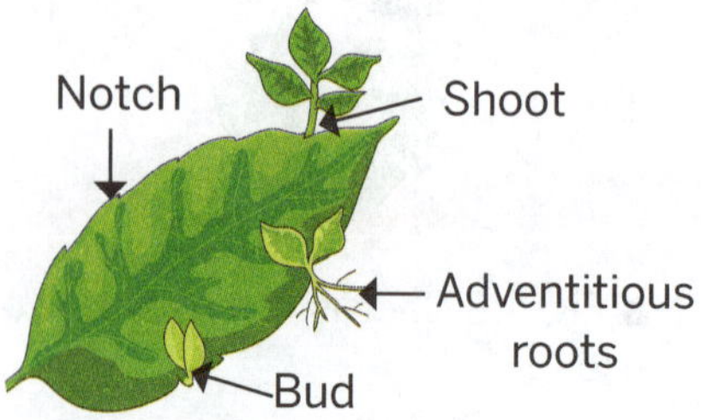

▲ Fig. 1.12 Vegetative propagation through a leaf

Activity 4

Aim: To carry out vegetative propagation through a *Bryophyllum* leaf

Procedure: Take a *Bryophyllum* leaf with some buds on the margin. Cut the leaf into small pieces such that each piece has some buds. Keep one piece in a pot containing soil. Water the soil everyday to keep it moist.

Observation: After a few days, new shoots can be seen coming out of the soil.

Flower

Flowers are the colourful parts of a plant. Flowers are found in all sizes. They develop from floral buds on the stem. Flowers grow to form fruits, fruits have seeds and seeds on sowing germinate into new plants. Hence, flowers play an important role in reproduction of a plant.

Parts of a Flower

A typical flower has four main parts.

- **Calyx**: It is the outermost covering of the flower and it is green in colour. It is made up of **sepals**. The calyx protects the flower in the early stages of development.
- **Corolla**: It is found next to the calyx. Brightly-coloured, scented **petals** of a flower form the corolla. Petals attract insects for pollination.

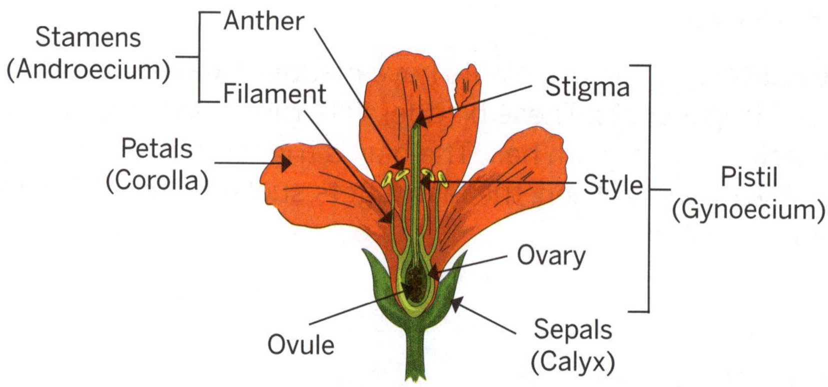

▲ Fig. 1.13 Parts of a flower

- **Androecium**: Stamens of the flower are collectively called the androecium. These are the male reproductive parts. Each stamen has a thin stalk called **filament** and a lobed structure called **anther**. The anther has fine, powdery structures called **pollen grains**.
- **Gynoecium (pistil)**: **Carpels** of a flower are collectively called the gynoecium. These are the female reproductive structures of the flower. Each carpel has three parts: (i) **Stigma** is the sticky part at the tip of the style. (ii) **Style** is the extended stalk, which connects the ovary to the stigma. (iii) **Ovary** is the swollen pistil base consisting of ovules.

Activity 5

Aim: To observe the parts of a flower

Materials required: A microscope, dissection needle, scissors, forceps, slide and hibiscus flower

Procedure:

1. Observe the sepals of the flower from the outside.
2. Select one side of the flower and cut off the petals using scissors and forceps to see the bulging shape of the ovary.
3. Cut open the ovary vertically using the needle towards the stigma to observe the ovary and the ovules.
4. Cut one of the anthers and place it on a drop of water on a slide.
5. Now, press the anther in the water so that the pollen comes out into the water.
6. Place a cover slip over the water and pollen grains to observe them using a microscope.

Observation: Observe all the parts of the flower using the reference figure of the flower in the textbook.

Functions of a Flower

- The reproductive system of a plant is found in the flowers.
- A flower attracts pollinators to facilitate pollination.
- It provides a platform for the development of fruits and seeds.

Pollination

Pollination is the transfer of pollen grains from the anther of a flower to the stigma of the same or different flower. Pollination is required for the formation of fruits and seeds.

Pollination can occur in two ways:

Self-pollination: Pollination occurring within the same flower or other flower of the same plant is called self-pollination.

Cross-pollination: Pollination occurring between two flowers of different plants of the same species is called cross-pollination.

▲ Fig. 1.14 Self-pollination and cross-pollination

Agents of Pollination

Wind, water, animals, birds and insects help in transferring pollen from the anther of one flower to the stigma of another. These are, therefore, called agents of pollination.

Pollination by insects: Brightly-coloured flowers attract insects. These flowers are usually big in size and highly scented. Bees and birds sit on flowers to collect nectar from flowers. Pollen gets stuck to their wings and legs. When they fly, the pollen falls on other flowers, thus, aiding pollination.

Pollination by wind: Field plants like maize, grass and paddy are pollinated through wind as the pollens are very light in weight and large in number. The stigma protrudes out in order to collect the pollen from the wind for fertilization.

Pollination by water: Aquatic plants like hydrilla have their pollen spread on the water surface. Flowing water carries the pollen to other flowers for pollination.

Pollination by birds and animals: The flowers provide food and nectar to many birds and small animals. In turn, the animals come in contact with the pollen that is carried on their body. When they visit another flower, the pollen on their body comes in contact with the stigma of the flower, leading to pollination.

▲ Fig. 1.15 Different agents of pollination

Fertilization

Mature pollen from an anther of a flower falls on the stigma of the same flower or another flower of the same kind by the aid of pollinating agents. Each pollen grain on the stigma then sends out a tiny, thread-like tube called a **pollen tube**. The tube grows down through the

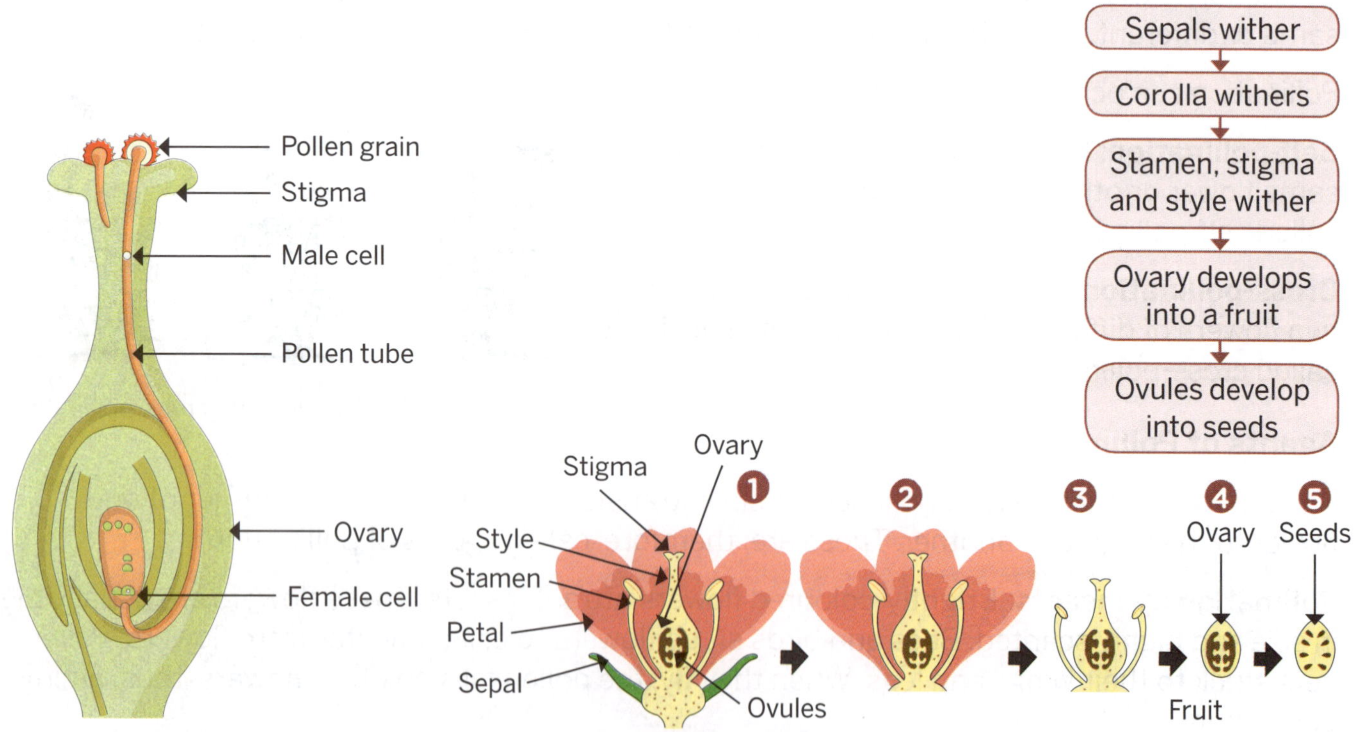

▲ Fig. 1.16 Fertilization and fruit formation

style and reaches one of the ovules in the ovary. In the ovary, the male cell in the pollen grain fuses with the female cell in the ovule. This process is called **fertilization**. In other words, fertilization can be defined as the fusion of male and female gametes of the flower. The fusion of the gametes forms a single cell called the **zygote**.

The zygote develops into a new plant later on. Ovules develop into **seeds**. The ovary forms the **fruit**. The sepals and the petals fall off.

Fruit

Fruit is the ripened ovary. Seeds are enclosed within fruits. A typical fruit consists of a **pericarp** (the fruit wall), which encloses the seed or seeds. The wall of the ovary develops into a pericarp. It can be dry or fleshy. In fruits like mango and avocado, the pericarp is differentiated into three layers.

- **Epicarp or Exocarp**: It is the outermost layer of the fruit. It is either thin or thick and is usually not eaten.
- **Mesocarp**: It is the middle layer of the fruit. It is sweet and fleshy, and is the edible portion of the fruit.
- **Endocarp**: It is the inner layer of the fruit. It is hard and encloses the seed in it.

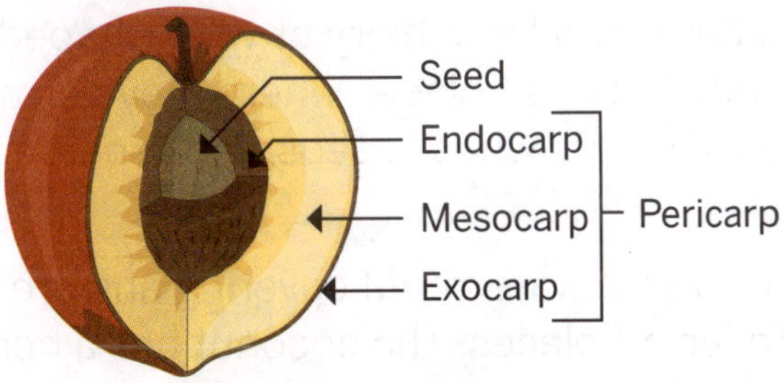

▲ Fig. 1.17 Parts of a fruit

> **Do You Know?**
>
> **Fruit Facts**
> - Carambola is a tree that bears star-shaped fruits.
> - Kiwi is also the name of a fruit with a brown exocarp, green mesocarp and black seeds.

Functions of a Fruit

- Fruit protects the seeds from different environmental conditions.
- It helps in the dispersal of seeds by animals, birds and wind.
- The seed has cotyledons which store food for the developing embryo.

Seed

Seeds are the fertilized, matured ovules. Fruits may have a single seed (for example, mango and plum) or many seeds (for example, apple and orange). Size and shape of the seeds vary from species to species.

The seed is protected by an outer covering called seed coat. Inside the seed coat, there are one or two **cotyledons**. The cotyledon stores food for the new plant or the embryo. An embryo consists of a **plumule** and a **radicle**. Under favourable conditions ,i.e., optimum supply of air, water, sunlight and temperature, the radicle develops into a root system and the plumule develops into a shoot system.

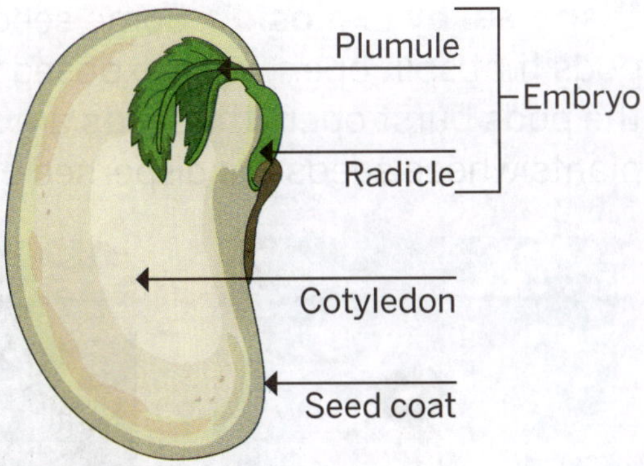

▲ Fig. 1.18 Parts of a seed

Depending on the number of seed leaves or cotyledons, seeds can be categorized as monocot (having one cotyledon) and dicot (having two cotyledons).

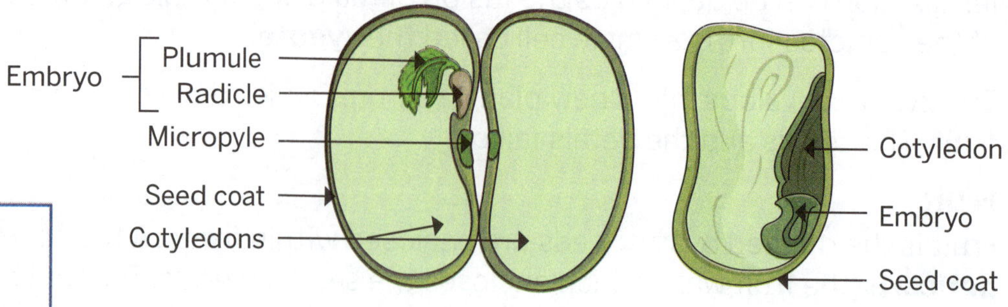

(a) Dicot (b) Monocot

▲ Fig. 1.19 Structure of a typical seed

Do You Know?

Strawberry and cashew are fruits that have their seeds on the outside.

Seed Dispersal

The process in which the seeds are scattered far away from the parent plant to obtain suitable conditions for germination is called **dispersal of seeds**. Seed dispersal is carried out in nature by wind, water and animals. They are also called **agents of dispersal**.

Dispersal by wind: Some fruits have very light, hairy or wing-shaped seeds that get caught in the wind and are easily blown away to far-off places where they germinate in fertile soil under favourable conditions. Examples of plants whose seeds are dispersed by wind are dandelion, cotton and maple.

Dispersal by water: Some fruits have a waterproof covering and are so light that they can float on water and are carried to far-off places. The coconut has a heavy seed inside, but it can still float on water because the seed is covered by spongy layers of fibre filled with air. Other examples of plants whose seeds are dispersed by water are lotus, water lily and foxglove.

Dispersal by animals: Some seeds have hook-like structures that help them to cling to animals' fur or sticky substances that stick to the animals' skin.

Many birds eat fruits along with their seeds. The seeds pass out of their bodies along with the undigested food and grow into new plants. Examples of plants whose seeds are dispersed by animals are cocklebur, mistletoe and berries.

Dispersal by explosion: Some seeds are covered with a leathery covering or are found inside pods that split open when exposed to the sun, when they dry up or even when touched. When the pods burst open, the seeds are scattered far away from the mother plant. Examples of plants whose seeds are dispersed by explosion are pea, gorse, peanut, balsam and castor.

(a) Dispersal by wind (dandelion)

(b) Dispersal by water (coconut)

(c) Dispersal by animals (cocklebur)

(d) Dispersal by explosion (peas)

▲ Fig. 1.20 Different types of dispersal of seeds

Seed Germination

The process by which the dormant (inactive) embryo inside the seed becomes active and begins to grow into a new plant is called **germination**. Moisture, oxygen and a suitable temperature are the conditions necessary for a seed to germinate.

During germination, the seed absorbs water and swells up, and the seed coat becomes soft and bursts open. The radicle grows downwards and becomes the primary root. The plumule grows upwards and becomes the primary shoot.

Germination can be of two types: epigeal and hypogeal.

Epigeal germination: This type of germination is usually seen in dicot seeds like beans. In such seeds, the cotyledons are pushed above the ground, become green and start to photosynthesize. They finally shrivel and fall off. The plumule then develops into the true leaves of the plant.

Hypogeal germination: This type of germination is usually seen in monocot seeds like wheat, maize and rice, and some dicot seeds like pea and gram. In such seeds, the cotyledon remains under the ground, and the food stored in it is used for growth of the plant.

(a) Epigeal (b) Hypogeal

▲ Fig. 1.21 Seed germination

Activity 6

Aim: To infer the conditions necessary for germination of seeds

Procedure:

Set-up 1:

1. Soak a few seeds in a bowl of water for about 30 minutes.
2. Dampen a cotton cloth with water and place it in a plastic bowl.
3. Place the soaked seeds in the plastic bowl and cover the bowl with foil paper.
4. Now, keep the bowl undisturbed in a dark place for two days.

Set-up 2:

1. Take a handful of seeds in a plastic container and add excess amount of water to it such that the seeds are floating in water.

2. Place the plastic container in direct sunlight.
3. Leave the set-up undisturbed for two days.

Set-up 3:

1. Take a handful of seeds in a plastic container.
2. Close the plastic container with a lid.
3. Keep the plastic container near a window.
4. Leave the set-up undisturbed for two days.

Experimental set-up	Conditions	Observation
Set-up 1		
Set-up 2		
Set-up 3		

Result: Optimum light, water and air are the necessary conditions for the germination of seeds.

Keywords

Nodes: the point on the stem from where a leaf or a branch arises

Venations: the arrangement of veins in plant leaves

Tendrils: modified stems or leaves for support, which appear as a coiled structure

Androecium: male reproductive part of a flower

Gynoecium: female reproductive part of a flower

Pollination: the transfer of pollen grains from the anther of a flower to the stigma of the same flower or another flower of the same species

Fertilization: the process of fusion of male and female gametes to form a zygote

In a Nutshell

- Leaves help in photosynthesis, exchange of gases and transpiration.
- Leaves are classified into simple and compound leaves.
- Most plants have one of the two types of venation in leaves: reticulate or parallel.
- The arrangements of leaves in the plants are whorled, opposite and alternate.
- Insectivorous plants have modified leaves that help in trapping insects.
- Flowers help in reproduction of plants.
- Flowers undergo pollination and fertilization to form seeds and fruits.
- The pollination and dispersal of seeds take place with the help of wind, water, insects, birds and animals.

Mind Map

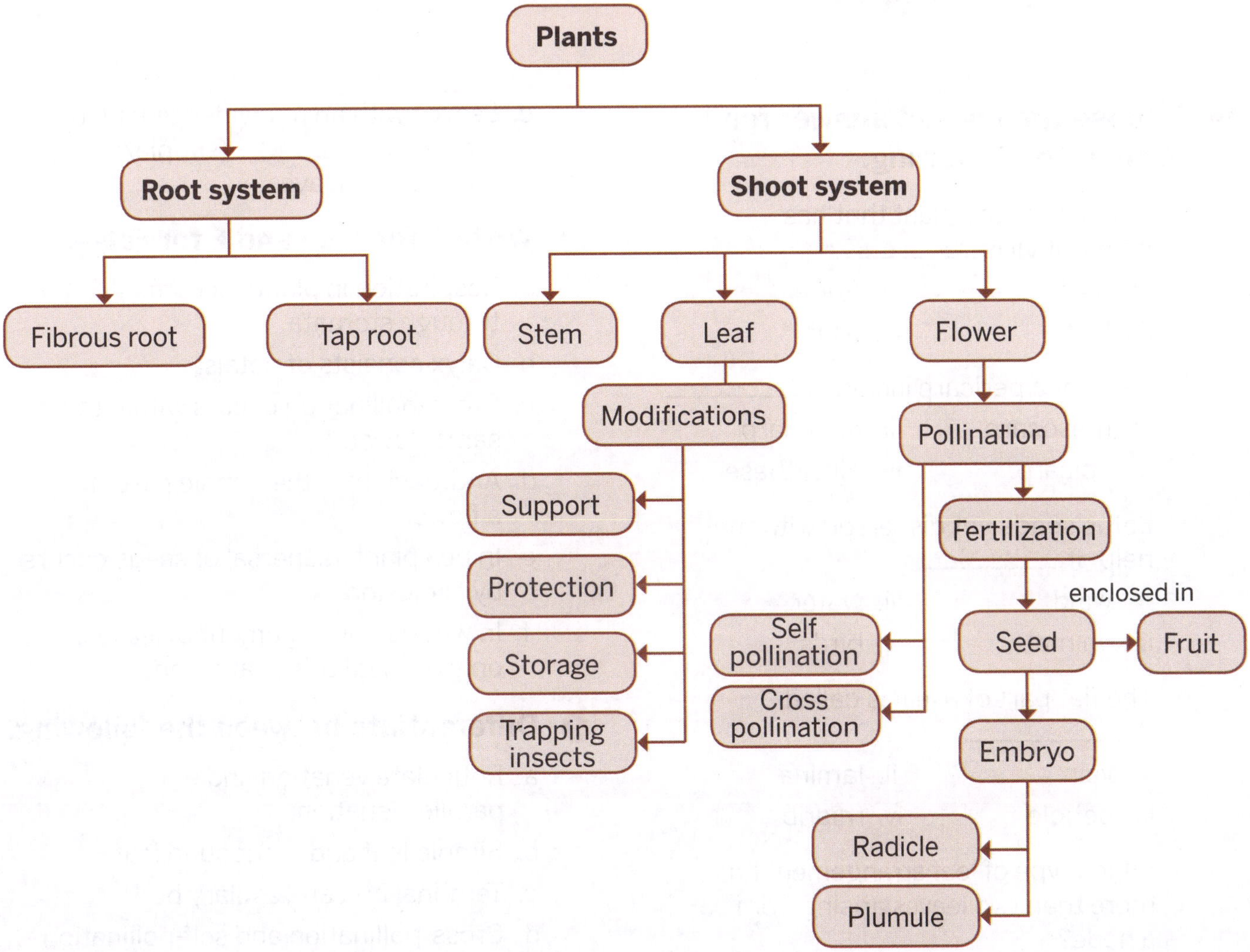

Plants
Root system
Shoot system
Fibrous root
Tap root
Stem
Leaf
Flower
Modifications
Support
Protection
Storage
Trapping insects
Pollination
Self pollination
Cross pollination
Fertilization
enclosed in
Seed
Fruit
Embryo
Radicle
Plumule

Exercise

1. Choose the correct answer for each of the following.

a. The part of the plant that has chlorophyll is ________.

i. root ii. flower

iii. leaf iv. fruit

b. Parts of a pericarp includes ________.

i. mesocarp ii. endocarp

iii. epicarp iv. all of these

c. Lotus seeds get dispersed with the help of ________.

i. wind ii. water

iii. animals iv. birds

d. The flat part of a leaf is called the ________.

i. vein ii. lamina

iii. petiole iv. midrib

e. Which type of leaf arrangement has more than two leaves arising from a node?

i. Alternate ii. Whorled

iii. Opposite iv. Reticulate

2. Fill in the blanks.

a. The male reproductive part of the flower in a plant is called ________ (androecium/gynoecium).

b. ________ (Stem/Leaf) is modified into spines in cactus.

c. In plants, oxygen is released during the process of ________ (respiration/ photosynthesis).

d. In ________ (parallel/reticulate) venation, veins are arranged in a net-like pattern on both sides of the midrib.

e. Leaves with an undivided leaf blade are called ________ (simple/ compound) leaves.

3. Write T for True and F for False.

a. Respiration in plants occurs through stomata.

b. Calyx consists of petals.

c. Cross-pollination occurs within the same flower.

d. Androecium is the female part of a flower.

e. In pea plant, dispersal of seeds occurs by explosion.

f. In whorled arrangement of leaves, only one leaf arises at a node.

4. Differentiate between the following.

a. Reticulate venation and parallel venation

b. Simple leaf and compound leaf

c. Terminal bud and axillary bud

d. Cross-pollination and self-pollination

e. Nodes and internodes

5. Answer the following questions in brief.

a. Name the different methods of seed dispersal.

b. What are the different types of leaf venations?

c. Explain the parts of a fruit with the help of a diagram.

d. What are the agents of pollination?

e. Define pollination.

f. Define fertilization.

g. What is seed dispersal?

6. **Answer the following questions in detail.**

a. Explain modifications in leaves.

b. What are the functions of fruits and flowers?

c. Draw a neat diagram of a flower and label its parts.

d. Explain the formation of fruits.

e. Explain the different modes of seed dispersal.

f. Explain the parts of a seed with a neat labelled diagram.

g. Briefly explain the process of seed germination.

7. **Think and answer.**

a. Other than green leaves, leaves of different colours are also seen in nature. What do you think might be the reason for different colours of the leaves? (Hint: Green leaves have chlorophyll pigment in them.)

b. After finding out the reason behind different colours of the leaves, check if these plants also have the green pigment (chlorophyll) in them and how these plants synthesize their food. (Hint: Photosynthesis)

8. **Thinking Beyond**

Soak different types of seeds. Let the seeds germinate. Check which type of germination is taking place-epigeal or hypogeal.

9. **Project**

a. Make a collage of different shapes of leaves and display it in the class.

b. Collect different types of seeds. Stick them on a chart paper. Identify the mode of seed dispersal and write few sentences about it.

Worksheet

❶ Subject Integration

Find out how each plant parts given below are adapted to the climatic conditions in different parts of the world and complete the table below.

Part of the plant	Subtropical arid climate	Tropical wet	Alpine region
Leaves			
Roots			
Flowers			
Fruits			
Stem			

❷ Life Skill

Plants give us food, medicines, raw materials for construction, textiles and so on. Plants also beautify our surroundings and purify the air.

Some plants (herbs) that can be grown in kitchen garden are listed below along with their germination and harvest times. Try growing some plants in your kitchen garden or in flower pots. Care for them and water them regularly.

Herb	Germination time	Harvest time	Herb	Germination time	Harvest time
Basil	5-10 days	10 weeks	Parsley	14-30 days	10-11 weeks
Chives	7-14 days	Varies	Peppermint	10-15 days	All year
Coriander	7-10 days	3-4 weeks	Rosemary	14-21 days	11-14 weeks
Lavender	14-21 days	Summer	Sage	7-21 days	11-13 weeks
Lemon balm	7-14 days	All year	Tarragon	10-14 days	11 weeks
Oregano	7-14 days	11-13 weeks	Thyme	14-21 days	13-14 weeks

The Cell

2

What I shall learn

- Discovery of cells
- Cell theory
- Diversity in cells
- Structures of animal and plant cells
- Structures and functions of cell organelles
- Cell division and growth

Know the Scientist

Robert Hooke (1635-1703), in his book, *Micrographia*, described his observations of cork cells viewed using his microscope with a magnification of 50x, through his magnificent drawings published in the book. He discovered cells.

Introduction

Biology is the study of living things. There are various kinds of living beings on Earth. Some can be seen with the naked eye, for example, plants and animals, and some cannot, for example, microorganisms.

A **cell** is the basic unit of life; therefore, cells are called the structural and functional units of an organism.

In this chapter, we will learn about the structure of cells and their functions.

Discovery of Cells

Cells were discovered only after the invention of microscopes.

In 1665, an English scientist named Robert Hooke discovered cells. He observed a thin slice of cork under his crude microscope made of two lenses (a compound microscope). He noticed tiny empty spaces enclosed by walls. He observed that they looked like compartments and hence, named them **cells** (derived from *cellula* in Latin meaning 'small compartment').

In 1670, a Dutch scientist named Antonie Van Leeuwenhoek developed a simple microscope using a single lens. He observed and described the cells in a drop of pond water using this microscope.

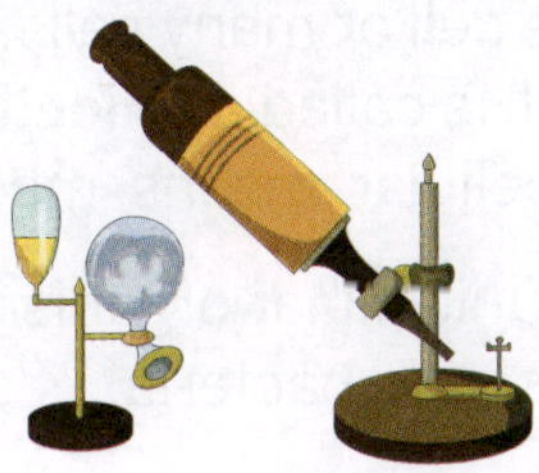

▲ Fig. 2.1 Hooke's microscope

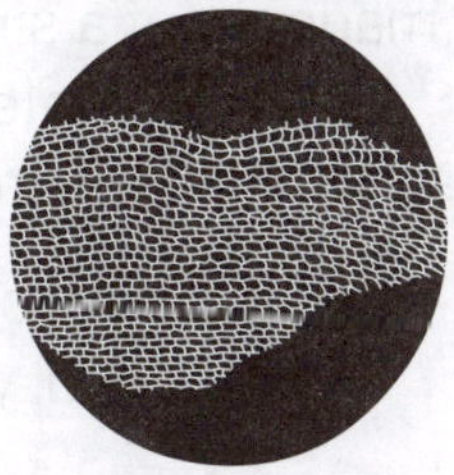

▲ Fig. 2.2 Cork cells observed by Hooke

▲ Fig. 2.3 Leeuwenhoek's microscope

Know the Scientist

Antonie Van Leeuwenhoek (1632–1723) is known as the father of microbiology. He created a simple light microscope with a magnification of upto 270x. He initially observed single-celled organisms. He called these tiny organisms, **animalcules**, which are now called **microorganisms**.

Tech Info

The world's most powerful microscope (weighing about 7 tonne and measuring about 4.5 m), the Scanning Transmission Electron Holography Microscope (STEHM), is present in the University of Victoria. It is the first microscope of its kind in the world. In 2013, gold atoms were viewed through this microscope at a resolution of 35 picometres. It is about 20 million times more powerful than human eyesight.

Cell Theory

In 1838, Matthias Jakob Schleiden, a German botanist, declared that the cell is the basic building block of all plant material.

In 1939, Theodor Schwann, a German biologist, declared that animal tissues are made up of cells and finally concluded that cell is the basic unit of life.

In 1958, Rudolph Virchow, popularly known as the father of pathology, discovered that living cells divide to form new cells.

The cell theory was developed on the observations of Hooke, Leeuwenhoek, Schleiden, Schwann, Virchow and others. The cell theory states:

- All living organisms are made up of one or many cells.
- Cell is the structural and fundamental unit of any functional living organism.
- New cells arise from older cells by division.

Diversity in Cells

Scientists observe and study living cells using microscopes as they help to magnify the objects that are difficult to see with the naked eye. Stains (dyes) are used to colour the cells as they help in getting a detailed look at the structure of the cells. From such studies, we now know that different living organisms vary in cell size, shape and number.

Variation in Cell Number

Living organisms may be made up of a single cell or many cells. An organism that is made up of a single cell is called a **unicellular** organism ('uni' means 'single' and 'cellular' means 'made up of cells').

▲ Fig. 2.4 Unicellular organism (*Amoeba*)

Examples of unicellular organisms are *Amoeba, Paramoecium, Euglena*, yeast and bacteria.

In a unicellular organism, a single cell performs all life functions including feeding, movement, respiration and reproduction.

An organism made up of many cells is called a **multicellular** organism ('multi' means 'many'). Examples of multicellular organisms are plants and animals, including human beings.

(a) A plant

(b) An animal

▲ Fig. 2.5 Multicellular organisms

Wonder!

In human beings, a newborn baby has approximately 26 million cells and an adult has 50 trillion cells.

Variation in Cell Shape

In most unicellular organisms, the cell is of a definite shape but some organisms like *Amoeba* (plural is *Amoebae*) keep changing their shape.

In multicellular organisms, cells become specialized to perform specific functions and exist in different shapes.

- **Nerve cells** are elongated as they need to carry messages to different parts of the body.
- **Muscle cells** are cylindrical and branched. They help in movement by contracting and relaxing.
- **Skin cells** are flat in shape so that they have a large surface area for protecting the body.
- **White blood cells** (WBC) present in the blood can change their shapes to help destroy germs in the body.
- **Sperm cells** need to swim long distances, so they have a wiggly tail to propel themselves.
- **Cells in plants** may be hexagonal, rectangular or spherical depending on their functions.

Do You Know?

The unicellular organism, *Amoeba*, does not have a definite shape; it keeps changing its shape. It has false feet called **pseudopodia** that are temporary projections made from the cell. Pseudopodia appear and disappear as the *Amoeba* moves or feeds.

Thinking Beyond

Are the cells in an elephant larger than that in a rat? No, because the size of the cells has no relation to the size of the organism.

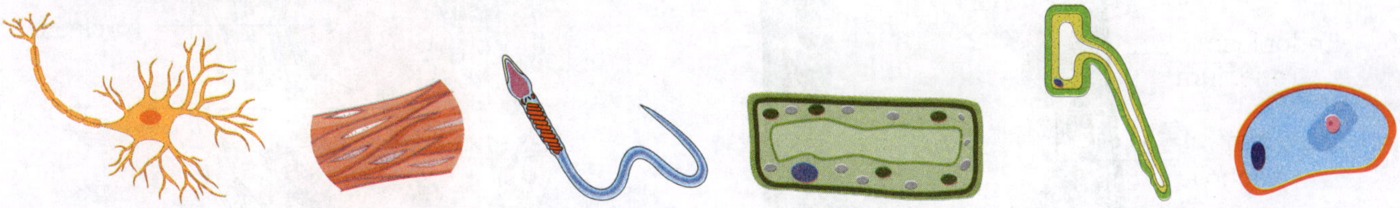

▲ Fig. 2.6 Variation in cell shape

Variation in Cell Size

Most cells are minute in size and are clearly visible only under a microscope. **Micron** or **micrometre** is the unit of measurement for cell size. One micron (μ) or one micrometre (μm) is equal to one millionth of a metre or one thousandth of a millimetre. It is mathematically represented as 1×10^{-6} m or 1/1,000,000 m.

Mycoplasma species of bacteria are the smallest living cells, measuring about 0.3 micrometres. **Nerve cells** are the longest cells in the human body, measuring about 0.1 millimetres. The giraffe has the longest nerve cell, measuring about 3 metres.

Revision Zone

Write T for True and F for False.

1. Antonie Van Leeuwenhoek viewed the cells of a thin slice of cork.
2. Cell theory states that new cells arise from division of older cells.
3. *Amoeba* cannot change its shape.
4. Nerve cells are the longest cells in the human body.
5. Micron or micrometre is the unit of measurement for cell size.

Structure of Cells

A cell has both living and non-living parts. The living parts present in a cell have a definite shape, structure and function, and are commonly called **organelles**. Typically, all cells (except bacteria) have three major parts—cell membrane, cytoplasm and nucleus. Plant cells have a cell wall, which surrounds the cell membrane. The cell wall is not found in animal cells.

Observe Fig. 2.7 carefully. We see that cell organelles are embedded in the cytoplasm. Each organelle present in the cell performs specific functions.

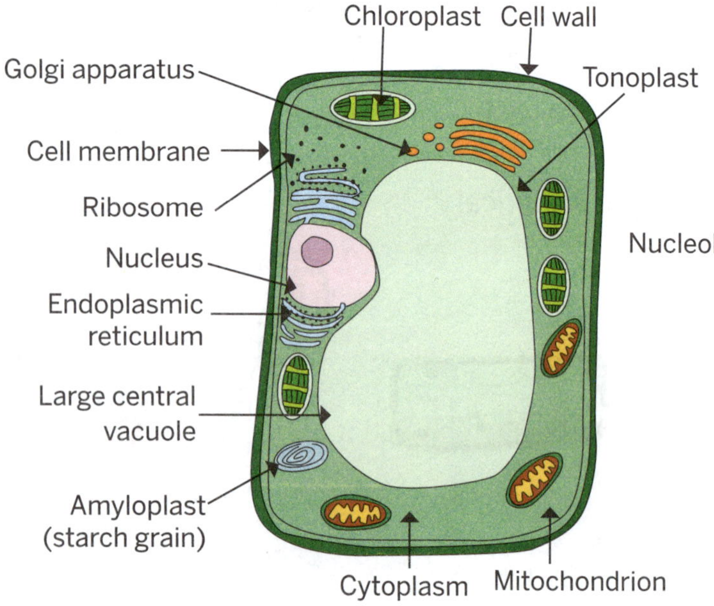

▲ Fig. 2.7 Plant cell

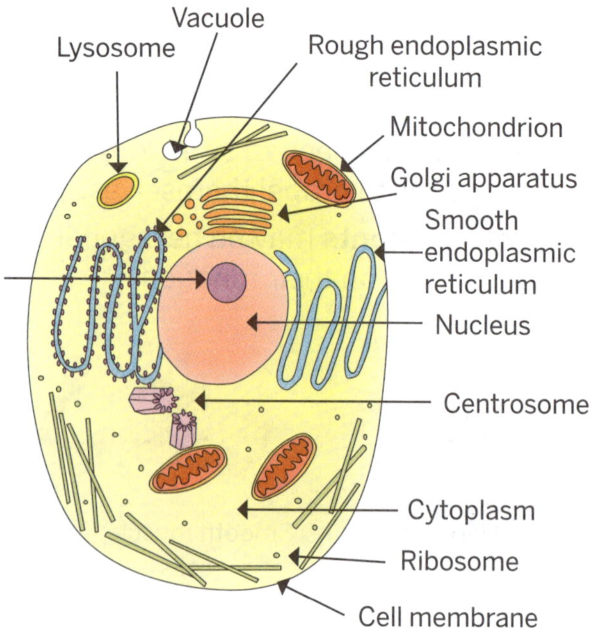

▲ Fig. 2.8 Animal cell

Let us learn about the parts of the cell and each of the cell organelles.

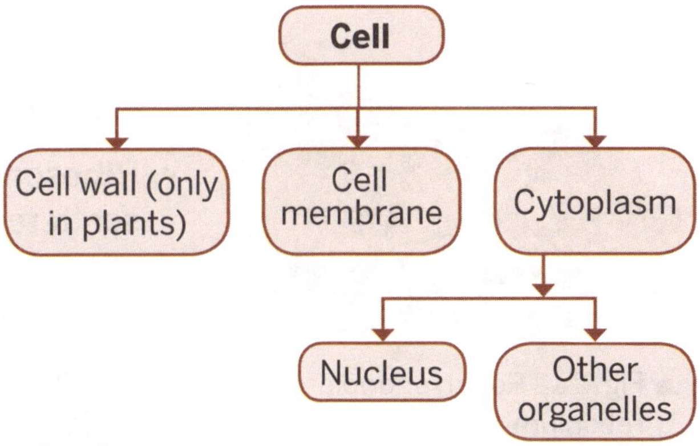

Cell membrane: A cell is surrounded by a thin covering called the **cell membrane** or the **plasma membrane**. The cell membrane protects the cell and gives it shape. It allows only selective movement of material in and out of the cell; hence, it is also called a **selectively permeable membrane**. It regulates the movement of selected substances like water and minerals, allowing them to enter and leave the cell.

Cell wall: The cell wall is present only in plant cells; animal cells do not have a cell wall. This extra layer provides rigidity and protection to the cells as plants do not have a skeleton for support. The cell wall is **completely permeable**, that is, it allows movement of all substances across it. The cell wall contains a large amount of **cellulose**.

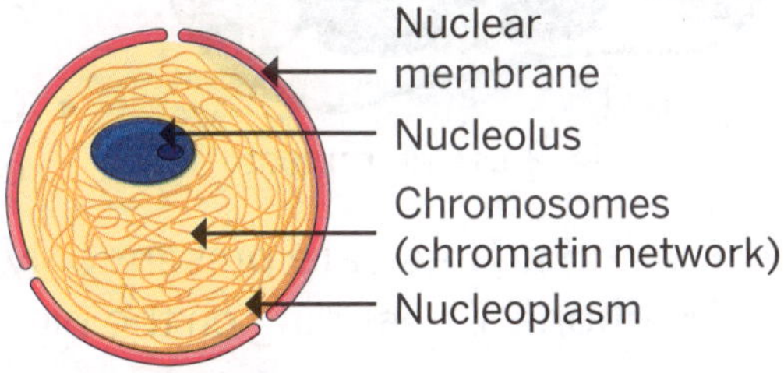

▲ Fig. 2.9 Parts of the nucleus

Nucleus: The nucleus controls the major functions of the cell. Thus, it is referred to as the brain of the cell. The nucleus is surrounded by a membrane called the **nuclear membrane**. A semi-solid substance called **nucleoplasm** is present inside the nucleus. The nucleoplasm contains thread-like substances called **chromosomes**. Chromosomes carry the hereditary material called **genes** that are responsible for transferring characteristics from parents to offspring. When a cell is not in a state of division, the chromosomes are seen as a network called **chromatin network**. A non-membrane bound, spherical structure called **nucleolus** is also present inside the nucleus.

Cytoplasm: Cytoplasm is the jelly-like fluid that is found within the cell membrane but outside the nucleus. Many organelles are embedded in the cytoplasm. Some cytoplasmic organelles are discussed below:

- **Golgi apparatus (Golgi bodies)**: It is made up of a stack of tube-like structures called **cisternae**, which are responsible for the secretion of chemical substances such as enzymes, hormones and proteins.
- **Mitochondria (singular: mitochondrion)**: These are small, rod-like or spherical structures. They oxidize food to provide energy and are, therefore, called the **powerhouse of the cell**.
- **Vacuoles**: These are sac-like structures enclosed by a membrane called **tonoplast**. They enclose a fluid called **cell sap**, which contalns excess water, food and wastes inside them. Plant cells have large vacuoles, whereas animal cells either do not have vacuoles or have very small vacuoles.
- **Lysosomes**: Lysosomes are found in animal cells. They contain chemical substances called **enzymes** that can digest cells and a variety of **intracellular** (found inside the cell) and **extracellular** (found outside the cell) material.

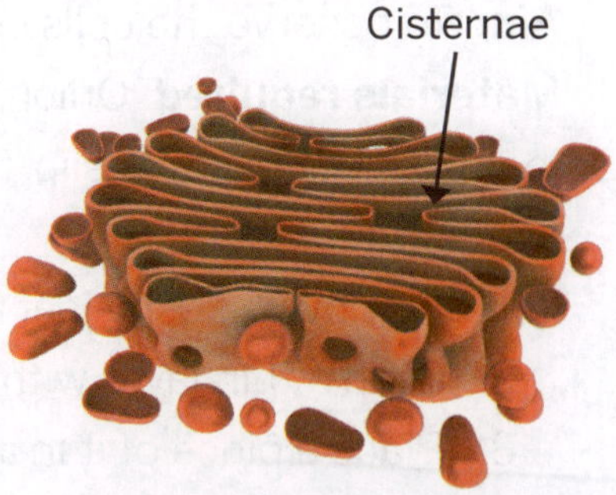

▲ Fig. 2.10 Golgi apparatus

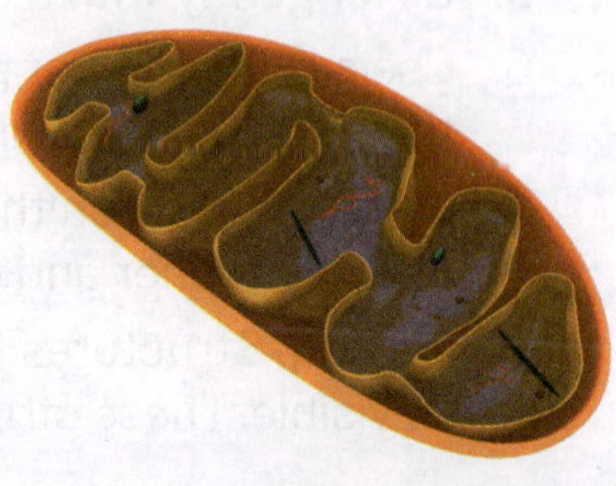

▲ Fig. 2.11 Mitochondrion

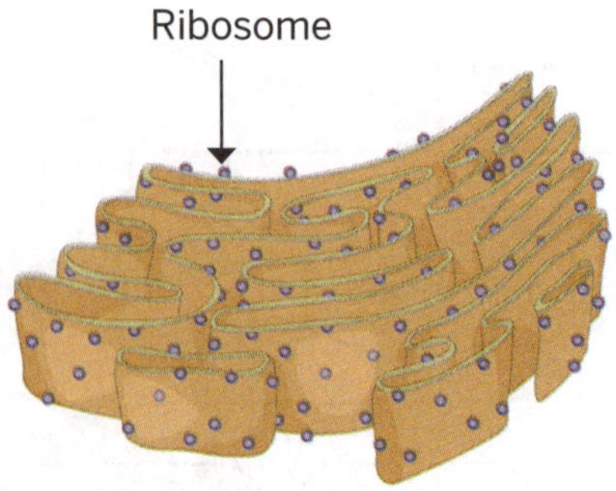

▲ Fig. 2.12 Rough endoplasmic reticulum

▲ Fig. 2.13 Chloroplast

During times of emergency, they release the enzymes which digest other cell organelles, thus killing the cell. Therefore, lysosomes are also called the **suicide bags** of the cell.

- **Ribosomes**: These are small, granular structures that are scattered in the cytoplasm and also found on the rough endoplasmic reticulum. Ribosomes are responsible for protein synthesis.
- **Endoplasmic reticulum (ER)**: It is a network of tubules, which are involved in storage and transportation of substances within the cell. There are two types of endoplasmic reticulum: **smooth ER** and **rough ER**. Rough ER has ribosomes attached to its surface due to which the surface has a grainy appearance. The smooth ER does not have ribosomes.
- **Centrosomes**: These structures are present only in animal cells. Centrosomes mainly initiate and regulate cell division.
- **Plastids**: These are present only in plant cells. Plastids contain **pigments** that have specific functions. Depending on the pigment present, plastids can be grouped into three types:

(a) **Chloroplasts**: These contain the green pigment called **chlorophyll**, which helps plants in carrying out photosynthesis.

(b) **Chromoplasts**: These contain non-green pigments that give colour to flowers and fruits.

(c) **Leucoplasts**: These are colourless and store food in the form of carbohydrates, proteins and fats. They mostly contain starch. Leucoplasts containing starch are called **amyloplasts**.

Activity 1

Aim: To observe the cells in an onion peel under a microscope

Materials required: Onion, forceps, watchglass, water, dropper, iodine solution, cover slip, filter paper and microscope

Procedure:

1. Remove a fleshy leaf from the onion bulb.
2. Strip a thin layer with forceps.
3. Place a piece of it in a drop of water on a clean side.
4. With a dropper, add a drop of iodine onto it.
5. Cover gently with a cover slip.
6. Use a piece of filter paper to remove excess liquid from the slide. Such a slide is known as a wet mount.
7. Place the slide on the microscope with the help of your teacher and observe.

Observation: Structures that look like bricks arranged side by side are visible. These structures are the cells of onion.

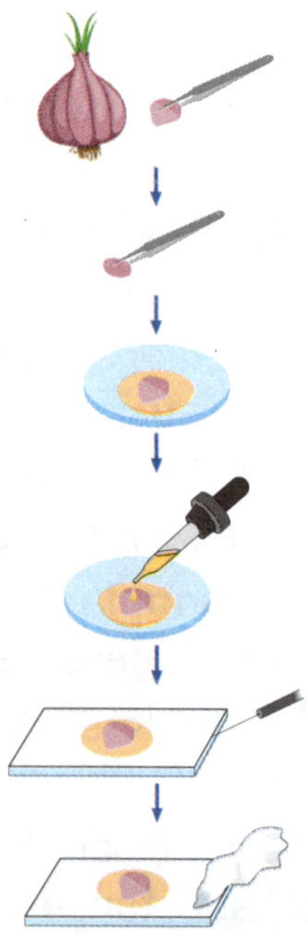

Steps for slide preparation

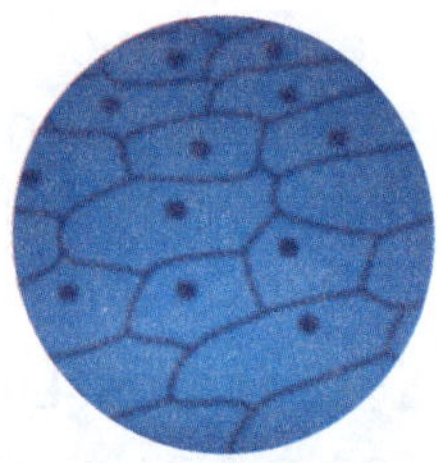

Cells seen under microscope

Activity 2

Aim: To observe cheek cells under a microscope

Materials required: Toothpick or swab, two glass slides, methylene blue stain, water, absorbent paper, cover slip and microscope

Procedure:

1. Gently scrape the inside of the cheek with a toothpick or swab.
2. Transfer the scraped tissue to a clean glass slide.
3. Bring the edge of another slide in contact with the scraped tissue and spread it out evenly on the first slide.
4. Prepare a thin smear.
5. Place a drop of methylene blue stain on the slide and spread across the entire slide.
6. Let the stain stay on the slide for two minutes.
7. Wash the slide gently with tap water to rinse off the excess stain.
8. Dab the slide with absorbent paper to take out the excess water.
9. Observe the cells under a microscope and verify that the cells are well-stained.
10. If necessary, apply the stain for a few minutes and repeat steps 7 and 8.
11. Place a cover slip over the stained cells. Tap the cover slip gently to spread the cells.
12. Observe the slide under the low power of the microscope.

Precautions:

1. Sterilize the material that you will use to swab.
2. Do not over stain the slide.
3. The smear should be very thin to avoid crowding of cells.

Observation: Tick (✓) the correct boxes.

Shape of the cells	Observation
Thin and flat	
Cube-shaped	
Ciliated	
Columnar (pillar-like)	
Oval	
Round	
Flat and scale-like	

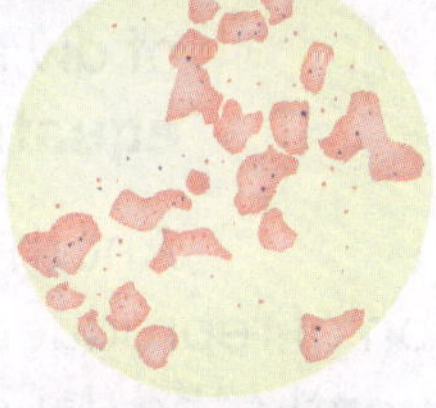

Cheek cells seen under microscope

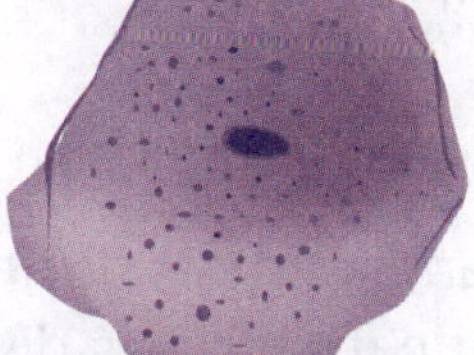

A single cheek cell

The major differences between plant and animal cells are given in Table 2.1.

Table 2.1 Differences between plant and animal cells

Feature	Plant cell	Animal cell
Cell wall	Present	Absent
Nucleus	Present at the edge of the cell; has nuclear membrane, nucleolus, nucleoplasm and chromosomes	Present at the centre of the cell; has nuclear membrane nucleolus, nucleoplasm and chromosomes
Vacuoles	Several in number; large and prominent	If present, small in size and few in number
Chloroplasts (Plastids)	Present	Absent
Centrosome	Absent	Present
Lysosome	Absent	Present

Revision Zone

Fill in the blanks.

1. Cell wall is seen in ____________ (animal/plant) cells.
2. ____________ (Nucleoplasm/Nucleolus) is a non-membrane bound, spherical structure present inside the nucleus.
3. ____________ (Chloroplast/Mitochondria) are called powerhouse of the cell.
4. Small, granular structures scattered in the cytoplasm, which are responsible for protein synthesis are called ____________ (ribosomes/mitochondria).

Cell Division and Growth

Once a cell is formed, it starts ingesting and digesting food, making the cell grow in size. The growth of a cell is limited. After reaching a certain size, it divides and forms new cells. The new cells formed in this manner are known as **daughter cells**.

During cell division, the nucleus (and the genetic material inside it) duplicates first. Then, the cytoplasm starts dividing. The daughter cells so formed are identical to each other and also to the parent cell, and have equal quantities of genetic material. Therefore, this kind of division is called **mitosis** or **equational division**.

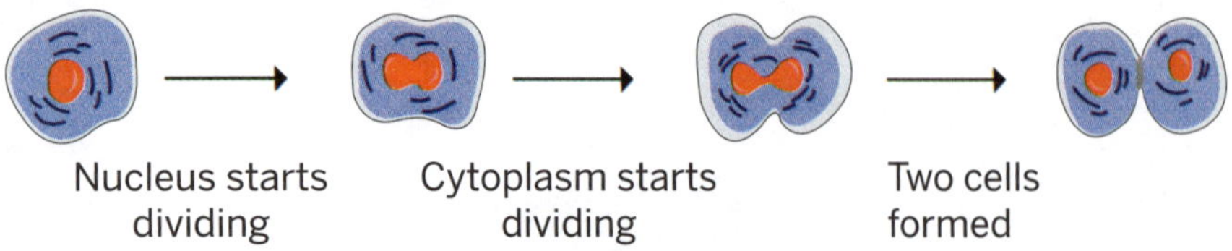

▲ Fig. 2.14 Cell division

Another kind of cell division occurs in higher plants and animals during the formation of reproductive cells or **gametes**. In this division, the genetic material is divided. Consequently, the daughter cells have half the amount of genetic material the parent cell had. Therefore, this type of division is called **meiosis** or **reductional division**.

Importance of Cell Division

Growth: Cell division is necessary for the growth of an organism. All multicellular organisms begin life as a single cell that divides repeatedly to give rise to new cells, thereby, leading to growth.

Replacing dead or damaged cells: New cells are also required to replace dying, damaged or worn-out cells in the body. During healing of wounds, damaged cells are replaced with new cells.

Reproduction: Cell division is required for production of reproductive cells or gametes.

Do You Know?

During cell division, sometimes mistakes occur in division of the genetic material. This results in changes called **mutations**, causing diseases like cancer and abnormal growth, including moles and non-cancerous tumours.

Keywords

Cells: basic structural and functional units of life

Unicellular organism: organism made up of a single cell

Multicellular organism: organism made up of many cells

Organelles: the living parts of a cell that possess a definite shape, structure and have specific functions

Gene: the part of a chromosome responsible for transfer of hereditary characteristics from the parents to the offspring

Tonoplast: membrane that surrounds the vacuole

Chloroplast: cell organelle present in plants that contain chlorophyll

Mitosis: cell division in which the genetic material in the nucleus duplicates and then separates into two parts with each part going to each of the two daughter cells

Meiosis: cell division in which the genetic material in the nucleus is divided equally between the daughter cells

In a Nutshell

- A cell is the structural and functional unit of life.
- Cells were discovered and named by Robert Hooke in 1665.
- In different organisms, cells show variations in number, shape and size.
- In unicellular organisms, a single cell performs all the life functions.
- In multicellular organisms, cells vary in shape and size according to the functions they perform.
- The basic structure of a cell consists of cell membrane, cytoplasm, nucleus and cell organelles.
- Cell membrane is selectively permeable. Plant cells have a cell wall in addition to the cell membrane.

- Various cell organelles are embedded in cytoplasm: Golgi apparatus, mitochondria, vacuoles, lysosomes, ribosomes, endoplasmic reticulum, etc.
- Golgi apparatus secretes enzymes, hormones and proteins, mitochondria oxidize food to release energy, vacuoles store cell sap, lysosomes digest intracellular and extracellular material, ribosomes synthesize proteins and endoplasmic reticulum stores and transports substances.
- Nucleus controls all the cell activities. It has the genetic material of the cell.
- Plant cells do not have lysosomes and centrosomes. Animal cells do not have cell wall, large vacuole and plastids.
- Cell division gives rise to new cells. It helps in growth, repair of worn out cells and reproduction.

Mind Map

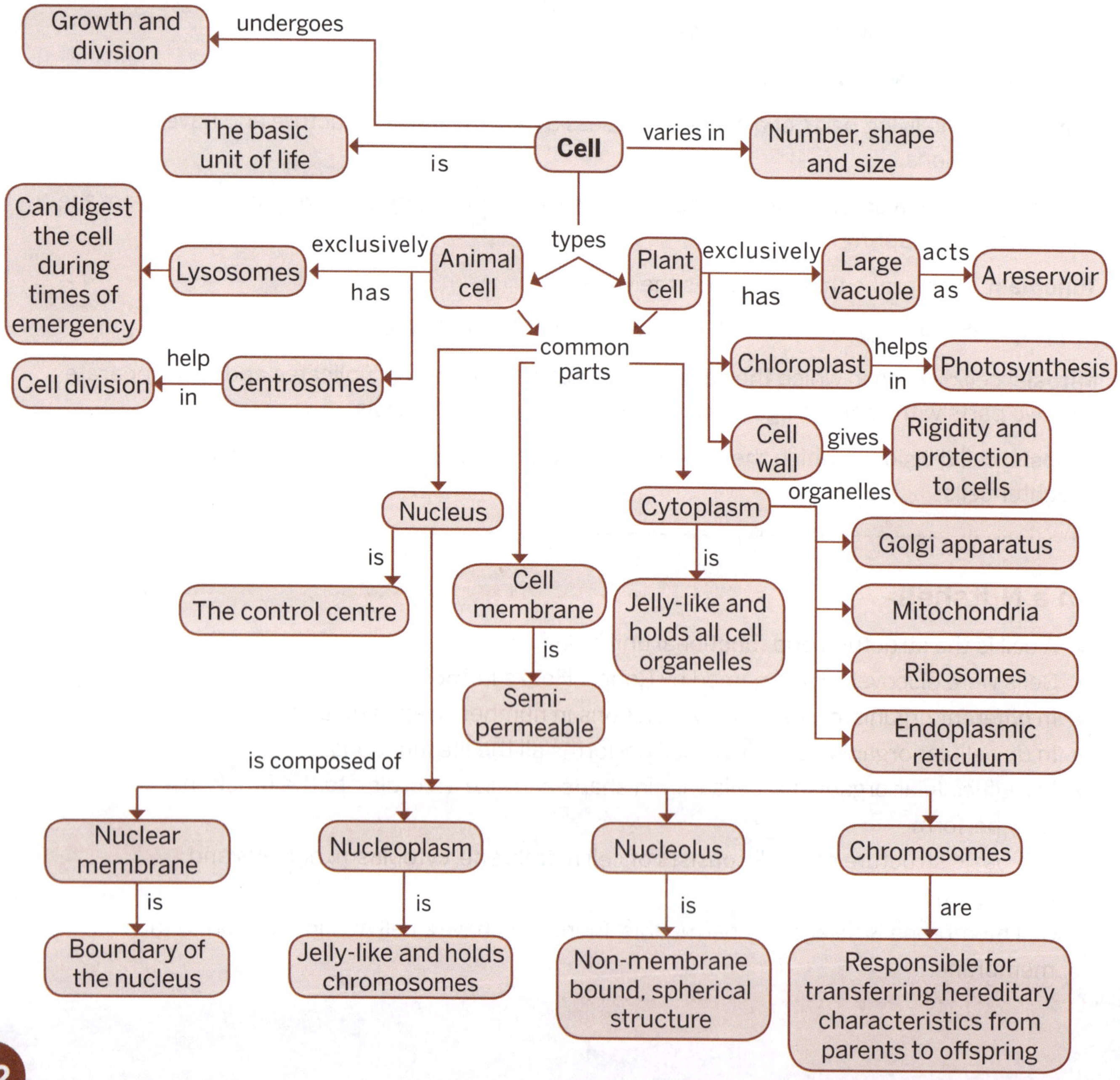

Exercise

1 Choose the correct answer for each of the following.

a. Who observed cork cells under a crude microscope?

i. Schwann ii. Schleiden
iii. Hooke iv. Leeuwenhoek

b. Which of the following is an example of a unicellular organism?

i. *Euglena* ii. Banyan
iii. Mosquito iv. Squirrel

c. One micron is equal to ____________ metre.

i. 1/1,000,000 ii. 1/100
iii. 1/1000 iv. 1/10

d. Which among the following is the longest cell?

i. Nerve cell ii. Pollen cell
iii. Muscle cell iv. Red blood cell

e. Cell organelles are embedded in ____________.

i. cytoplasm ii. cell membrane
iii. nucleoplasm iv. lysosomes

f. Which of the following is a selectively permeable membrane?

i. Cell membrane ii. Cell wall
iii. Both (i) and (ii) iv. None of these

g. The function of chloroplast is to

i. store food
ii. prepare food
iii. transport food
iv. break down food

h. These are called the powerhouse of the cell.

i. Mitochondria ii. Ribosomes
iii. Nucleus iv. Cytoplasm

i. Identify the organelle that is found in a plant cell but not in an animal cell.

i. Nucleus ii. Mitochondria
iii. Ribosome iv. Chloroplast

j. Which of the following is not a cell organelle?

i. Vacuole ii. Ribosome
iii. Chlorophyll iv. Plastids

2 Fill in the blanks.

a. ____________ (Tissue/Cell) is the structural and functional unit of life.

b. The living parts of a cell having a definite shape, structure and function and are called ____________ (organelles/organs).

c. The structures that help in transferring characteristics from parents to offspring are ____________ (genes/ vacuoles).

d. The jelly-like substance in which the organelles are embedded is called ____________ (centriole/cytoplasm).

e. The term 'cell' was first coined by ____________ (Robert Hooke/ Leeuwenhoek).

f. The membrane that encloses vacuoles is called ____________ (cell membrane/tonoplast).

g. Nucleoplasm and nucleolus are enclosed inside the ____________ (mitochondrial/nuclear) membrane.

h. Mitosis is also called ____________ (reductional/equational) division.

3 Write T for True and F for False.

a. Animal cells have a cell wall in addition to the cell membrane.

b. Mitochondria are called the protein factory of the cell.

c. Nuclear membrane is absent in plant cells.
d. Leucoplast is a type of plastid.
e. Vacuoles are prominent in plant cells.
f. Size and shape of cells remain same in all organisms.

4 Differentiate between the following.

a. Unicellular and multicellular organisms
b. Cell membrane and cell wall
c. Plant cell and animal cell
d. Smooth ER and Rough ER

5 Answer the following questions in brief.

a. Define cell. How were cells discovered?
b. State the cell theory.
c. Briefly explain the structure of the nucleus of a cell with the help of a diagram.
d. What is the function of lysosomes in an animal cell?
e. How are daughter cells formed?
f. What is the importance of cell division?

6 Answer the following questions in detail.

a. Discuss the variation in cell size, shape and number.
b. Explain the structure of an animal cell.
c. Draw a neat and labelled diagram of a plant cell and describe the structures.
d. Differentiate between a plant cell and an animal cell.
e. Write a brief note on the discovery of cells.
f. Give the steps involved in preparing a slide of onion cells to be viewed under a microscope.

7 Think and answer.

Which organism is functionally more effective: a unicellular organism where one single cell performs all the functions or a multicellular organism where different organs perform different functions? Give reasons.

(Hint: All life functions must be performed for survival.)

8 Project

Make an edible animal cell model using candy, gelatin and other edible ingredients.

Method: Prepare gelatin (to represent cytoplasm) as per the package instructions to form the cytoplasm of the cell. Pour it into a bowl (to represent the cell membrane) when slightly cooled and chill it until it is partially set. Once the gelatin reaches a thickened but soft stage, add candies of different shapes to the cell to represent the organelles. Use a fruit cut in half to represent the nucleus (the pit is the nucleolus and the skin is the nuclear membrane). Press the candies slowly into the setting gelatin to get a firm model. Finally, let the gelatin set until it becomes firm.

9 Thinking Beyond

All multicellular organisms start life as a single cell, which divides to give rise to more cells. Some cells specialize to perform specific functions. When such cells divide, they form cells of their own particular type. However, some cells have the capability to specialize into any of the different cell types in the body. These cells are called stem cells.

Stem cells are of special interest to scientists. Find out why.

Worksheet

❶ **Using the words given in the box, fill in the blanks in the flowchart below.**

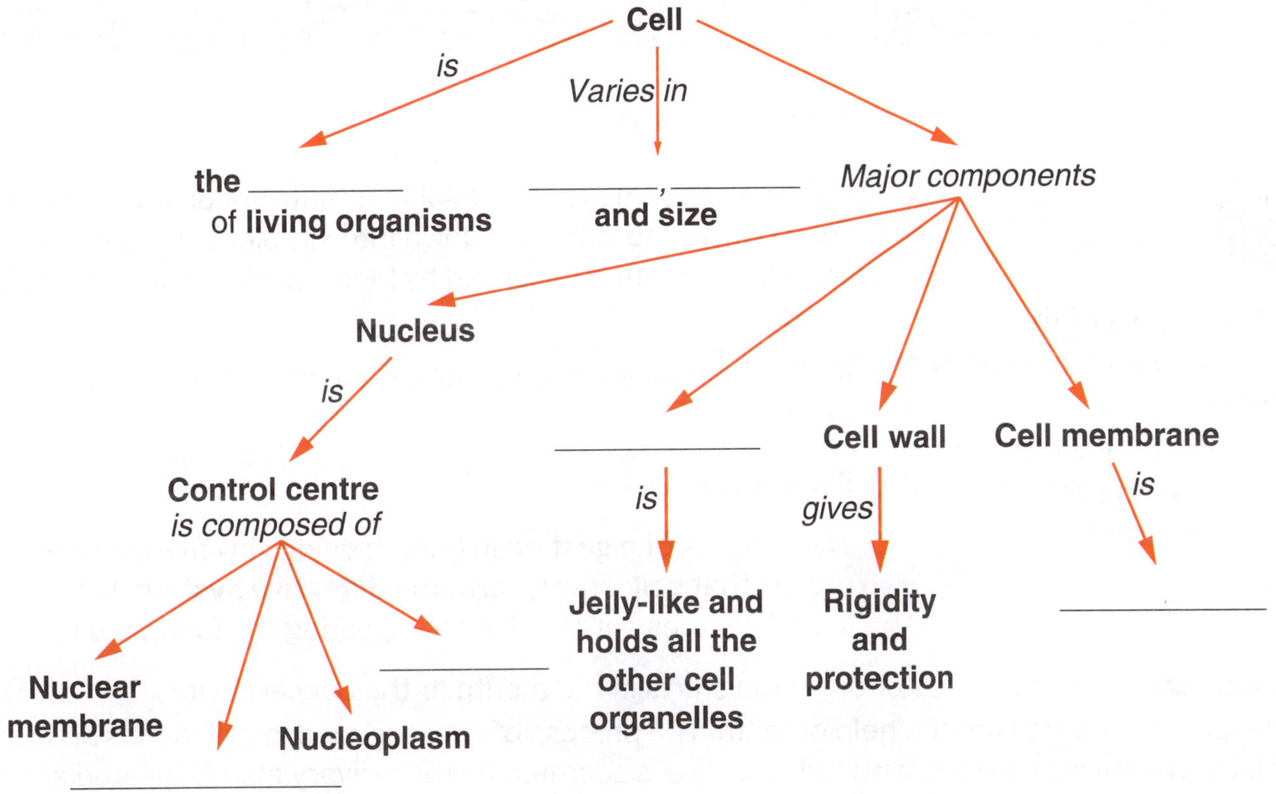

❷ **Label the following structures in the diagram of a generalized cell given below. Nucleus, Nucleolus, Mitochondria, Cell membrane, Cytoplasm, Endoplasmic reticulum**

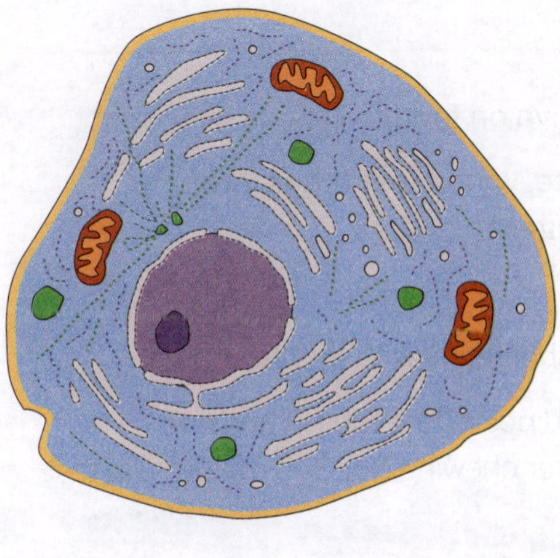

Human Body: Digestive System

3

What I shall learn

- Main organs of the digestive system and their functions
- Process of digestion of nutrients: carbohydrates, proteins and fats

Introduction

Animals consume food to fulfil their nutritional requirements. Food consumed is broken down into simpler substances by the digestive system and carried by blood to each and every cell of the body.

In this chapter, let us study about the process of digestion in detail.

Digestion

The process of digestion in human beings involves various organs that collectively form the **digestive system**. Let us learn how these organs help in digesting the food we eat.

Buccal cavity: The process of digestion starts in the mouth or the buccal cavity. The food is chewed with the help of teeth. The process of chewing food is called **mastication**. The tongue mixes the food with saliva. Saliva is secreted by the salivary glands located around the throat and in the mouth. The salivary glands secrete digestive juices that contain an enzyme called **salivary amylase**, which breaks down starch in the food to maltose.

$$\text{Starch} \xrightarrow{\text{Salivary amylase}} \text{Maltose}$$

Starch is a carbohydrate present in food in high quantities. We can understand the effect of saliva on food by performing the following activity.

Activity 1

Aim: To study the effect of saliva on food

Materials required: Boiled rice, water, test tubes, dropper, water bath and Benedict's reagent

Procedure:

1. Take two test tubes and label them as 'A' and 'B'.
2. Put one teaspoon of boiled rice in test tube A and one teaspoon of boiled rice after chewing (for 3–5 minutes) in test tube B.
3. Add 3–4 m of water to each of the test tubes.

A
Boiled rice with water

Boiled rice, water and Benedict's reagent after heating

4. Use a dropper to add 3–4 drops of Benedict's reagent to both the test tubes. Heat the test tubes for 10 minutes in a water bath.

Observation: In test tube A, there is no colour change in the solution. In test tube B, the colour of the solution changes to brick red.

Conclusion: Benedict's reagent turns brick red if sugar is present in a solution. As saliva breaks down the starch present in food into simple sugars (maltose), the test for sugar is positive in test tube B.

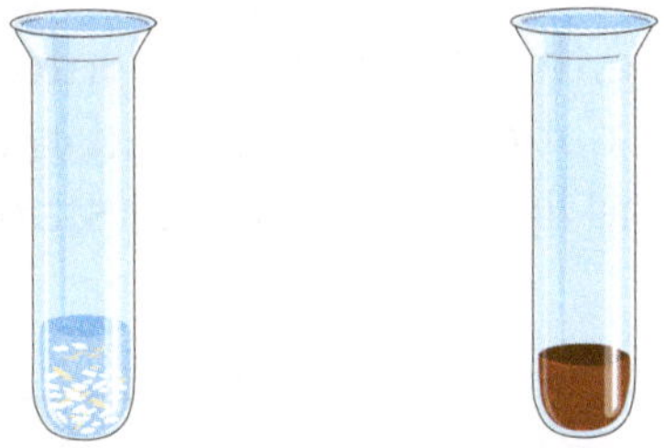

Oesophagus: The oesophagus is also called the food pipe. It is a long, muscular, tube-like structure that moves in a wave-like manner to push down food into the stomach. This movement is called **peristalsis**. The food is transported from the buccal cavity through the oesophagus to the stomach.

The movement of food through the alimentary canal (the passage along which food passes through the body during digestion) happens due to the peristaltic movement.

Stomach: The stomach is a muscular, sac-like organ. The inner lining wall of the stomach produces dilute hydrochloric acid and digestive juices containing the enzymes pepsin and rennin. Dilute hydrochloric acid kills the microbes that enter with the food. The enzyme pepsin helps in breaking down proteins into smaller molecules called **peptones**. The enzyme rennin works on the milk protein casein and converts it into curd.

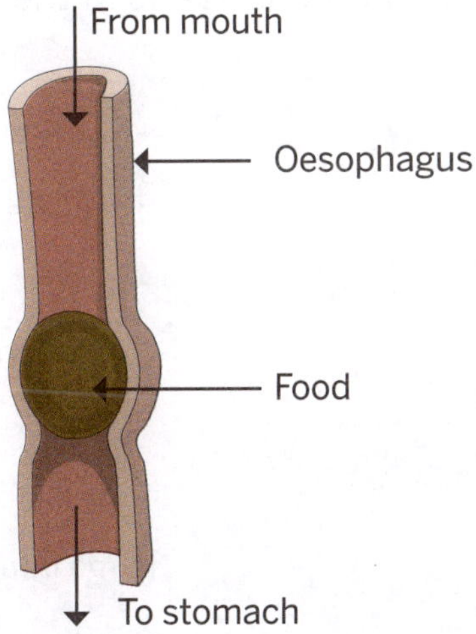

▲Fig. 3.1 Peristalsis

$$\text{Proteins} \xrightarrow{\text{Pepsin}} \text{Peptones}$$

$$\text{Casein} \xrightarrow{\text{Rennin}} \text{Curd (paracasein)}$$

The mucus membrane of the stomach keeps the inner wall of the stomach safe from the harmful effects of the acids. The food that is partially digested in the stomach is called **chyme**. This passes into the small intestine.

Liver: It is the largest gland in the body. It produces bile juice that helps in the digestion of fats. Bile juice is stored in a small, sac-like organ called the **gall bladder** below the liver. The bile juice from the gall bladder is secreted into the small intestine.

Small intestine: The chyme enters the first part of the small intestine called **duodenum** where most of the chemical breakdown of food takes place. Duodenum mixes the bile,

Science in Context

A small, flap-like organ called the **epiglottis** prevents the food from entering the trachea and channels it into the oesophagus. That is why, when you try to talk with your mouth full, you often choke as the food enters the trachea.

gastric and pancreatic juices, and bile salts from the gall bladder. The bile juice helps in converting the fat in the food into tiny droplets so that enzymes can work easily on them. The pancreatic juice produced in the pancreas contains digestive enzymes such as amylase, trypsin and lipase that digest starch, proteins and fats, respectively.

$$\text{Starch} \xrightarrow{\text{Amylase}} \text{Maltose}$$

$$\text{Proteins} \xrightarrow{\text{Trypsin}} \text{Peptides}$$

$$\text{Fats} \xrightarrow{\text{Lipase}} \text{Fatty acids and glycerol}$$

Here, the food being acted upon by the digestive juices is in the liquid form. Most of the digestion happens in the small intestine.

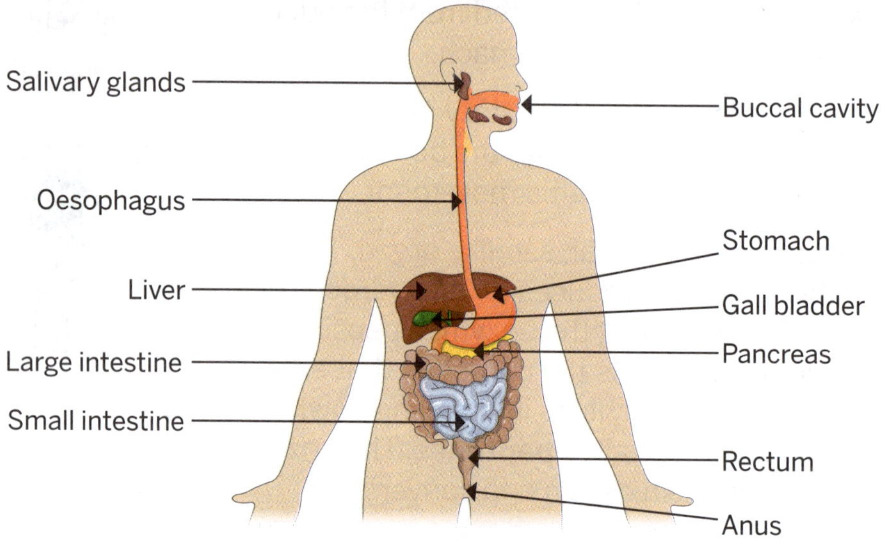

▲ Fig. 3.2 Human digestive system

The chyme now enters the second part of the small intestine called **jejunum** and the third part of the small intestine called **ileum** where the digestion is completed by the action of enzymes—erepsin, maltase, sucrase and lactase—secreted by the walls of the intestine. Erepsin converts peptides into amino acids. Maltase converts maltose into glucose. Sucrase converts sucrose into glucose and fructose. Lactase converts lactose into glucose and galactose.

$$\text{Peptides} \xrightarrow{\text{Erepsin}} \text{Amino acids}$$

$$\text{Maltose} \xrightarrow{\text{Maltase}} \text{Glucose}$$

$$\text{Sucrose} \xrightarrow{\text{Sucrase}} \text{Glucose + Fructose}$$

$$\text{Lactose} \xrightarrow{\text{Lactase}} \text{Glucose + Galactose}$$

Revision Zone

Write T for True and F for False.

1. Peptides get converted to amino acids in the presence of pensin.
2. The chyme first enters the part of the small intestine called duodenum.
3. Lactase enzyme acts on lactose and gives glucose and fructose as end products.
4. Maltose is obtained when salivary amylase acts on a starch molecule.

Absorption

The inner walls of the small intestine have finger-like projections called **villi** (singular: villus). These villi increase the surface area of the inner walls for absorption of digested food. Each villus has a network of blood vessels, which absorb the nutrients from the digested food.

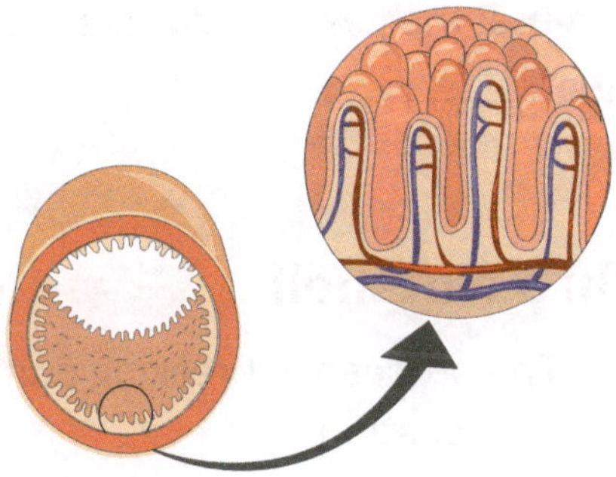

▲ Fig. 3.3 Villi on inner walls of small intestine

Assimilation

When the digested food, transported by blood to all the body cells, is either converted into products necessary for them or else utilized for their activities, it is called **assimilation**. This happens in all the cells of the body including the cells of the alimentary canal.

Glucose, which is the final product of carbohydrate digestion, is broken down with the help of oxygen into carbon dioxide and water to release energy. Amino acids are used for growth and repair of worn-out cells. Fatty acids and glycerol are stored below the skin as energy reserves.

Challenge Yourself

1. What happens to the glucose inside the cells of a person who is starting to jog?
2. What happens to the glucose inside the cells of a person who is always inactive, sitting and watching television?

Egestion

The undigested and unabsorbed food moves into the large intestine to a part called **colon** where some amount of water and salts are absorbed from the undigested food.

The remaining undigested food then moves to the second part called **rectum**. Here, it is stored and released from the body through the anus. This process is known as **egestion**.

Keywords

Digestion: the process of chemically breaking down complex food into its simple, soluble form

Absorption: the process of taking in digested food by the blood stream

Assimilation: the process by which the body uses the absorbed food for energy generation and growth

Egestion: removing or ejecting undigested food materials from the anus

Enzyme: a chemical that acts like a catalyst, specific in action, but is not used up during the process

Peristalsis: the process of contraction and relaxation of the food pipe or oesophagus

Chyme: the partially digested, semi-liquid food after passing through the stomach

In a Nutshell

- The process of breaking complex food substances into simple, soluble forms is known as digestion.
- The process of contraction and relaxation of the oesophagus is known as peristalsis.
- The process of digestion starts in the mouth and ends in the small intestine.
- Absorption is taking up of the digested food by the blood stream.
- When the digested food, transported by blood to all the body cells, is either converted into products necessary for them or else utilized for their activities, it is called assimilation.
- Excess water is reabsorbed by the capillaries surrounding the large intestine.

Exercise

1 Choose the correct answer for each of the following.

a. Stomach secretes
   i. bile juice
   ii. hydrochloric acid
   iii. pancreatic juice
   iv. amylase

b. Which of these break fat complexes?
   i. Amylase ii. Pepsin
   iii. Trypsin iv. Lipase

c. Bile is produced in
   i. liver ii. intestine
   iii. mouth iv. stomach

d. Breaking down food into simple, soluble substances is called
   i. absorption ii. digestion
   iii. egestion iv. assimilation

e. In the small intestine, proteins are digested by
   i. pepsin ii. renin
   iii. casein iv. trypsin

f. Food moves from the oesophagus to the stomach by
   i. swallowing ii. peristalsis
   iii. pumping iv. None of these

2 Fill in the blanks.

a. Duodenum is a part of the ____________ (stomach/intestine).

b. Undigested food must be ____________ (egested/reabsorbed).

c. Under the skin ____________ (fat/protein) is stored as reserve energy.

d. The process of taking up digested nutrients into the blood stream is called ____________ (assimilation/absorption).

e. The process of chewing food is called ____________ (mastication/digestion).

f. Sucrase changes sucrose into glucose and ____________ (fructose/galactose).

g. ____________ (Cilia/Villi) are finger-like projections on the inner walls of the small intestine.

3 Write T for True and F for False.

a. Ingestion is breaking down of food into simpler substances.

b. Egestion takes place through the small intestine.

c. Digestion takes place majorly in the large intestine.

d. Bile helps to digest protein.

e. Salivary amylase breaks down maltose into starch.

f. Amino acids are assimilated to form fat.

g. Villi are small projections in the stomach wall.

h. Digestive juice produced by the stomach contains hydrochloric acid.

i. Pancreatic juice contains enzymes to digest protein.

4 Answer the following questions in one sentence.

a. What is peristalsis?

b. What is the function of saliva in digestion of food?

c. What is chyme?

d. How does bile help in digesting fat?

5 Answer the following questions in brief.

a. Explain the role of amylase in digestion of food.

b. What is the function of hydrochloric acid secreted by the stomach?

c. What happens during assimilation?

6 Answer the following questions in detail.

a. Write the functions of the following organs of the digestive system: mouth, stomach, liver, small intestine, pancreas

b. List the parts of the small intestine and their functions.

c. Explain the human digestive system with the help of a labelled diagram.

d. List the enzymes secreted by different parts of the digestive system and explain their role in the digestion of food.

7 Think and answer.

Why does your stomach grumble when you are hungry?

8 In the Library

Food products like probiotic yoghurt have become popular nowadays. Find out what the term 'probiotic' means and how such products are beneficial for our digestive system.

9 Project

1. Talk to your family doctor and find out the symptoms and causes of indigestion. Also find out the ways to prevent or treat indigestion. Make a report on your findings.
2. Interview three people in your neighbourhood and find out their food habits. Also ask them if they have any problems related to the digestive system. Can you find a relation between the type of food eaten and the functioning of the digestive system?

Worksheet

Subject Integration

❶ **Label the different organs of the digestive system in the figure given below. Also, write the name of the enzyme secreted next to the name of the organ.**

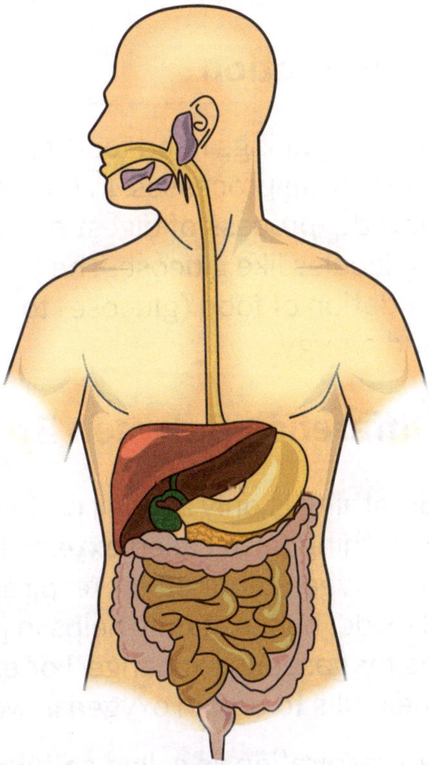

❷ **Unscramble the jumbled words that are the names of the parts of the human digestive system.**

a. CBUALC IVCYAT ____________________

b. ASPCRAEN ____________________

c. ALLMS ENITSETNI ____________________

d. HTMSACO ____________________

e. GREAI STEITENNI ____________________

f. SPSHEAOGUO ____________________

g. LAGL DBEARDL ____________________

h. SUAN ____________________

i. UGOENT ____________________

j. IRVLE ____________________

Human Body: Respiratory System

4

What I shall learn

- Difference between respiration and breathing
- Main parts of the respiratory system and their functions
- Mechanism of breathing
- Common respiratory diseases

Introduction

All living beings need food as a source of energy to carry out various life processes. In the previous chapter, we learned how the process of digestion breaks down food into simple molecules like glucose. The process of respiration involves the oxidation of food (glucose) to produce water, carbon dioxide and energy.

Difference Between Breathing and Respiration

Breathing is only a small part in the process of respiration. Breathing (also called **external respiration**) helps to obtain the oxygen required for respiration and gives out carbon dioxide; hence, it only helps in gaseous exchange. Different animals have various mechanisms for gaseous exchange. For example, human beings breathe through their nose and fish use their gills to obtain oxygen in water.

The next step, an important part of respiration, is called **cellular respiration** or **internal respiration**. It involves the breakdown of glucose in the presence of oxygen in the cells. This results in the release of water, carbon dioxide and energy in the form of ATP.

Table 4.1 Differences between breathing and respiration

Breathing	Respiration
No energy is obtained by the body	Energy is obtained from food
It is a mere exchange of gases between the atmosphere and the body	Respiration takes place within the cells of the body
It is a physical process involving breathing-in and breathing-out	A lot of biochemical processes happen when respiration is carried out in the cells

The Human Respiratory System

The organs of the human respiratory system are shown in Fig. 4.1 (given on the next page).

When air is inhaled, it passes through our nostrils and enters the **nasal cavity**. From the nasal cavity, the air enters the windpipe (**trachea**). The windpipe branches into two smaller tubes called **bronchi** (singular: bronchus). Each bronchus enters into a lung. In the **lungs**, each bronchus branches out into smaller tubes called **bronchioles**. At the end of these tubes, there are tiny air sacs called **alveoli** (singular: alveolus). The walls of the alveoli are lined with a network of blood vessels and capillaries to facilitate the exchange of gases. Lungs are present in the chest cavity, which is surrounded by ribs on the sides. The ribs form a cage-like structure called the **ribcage**.

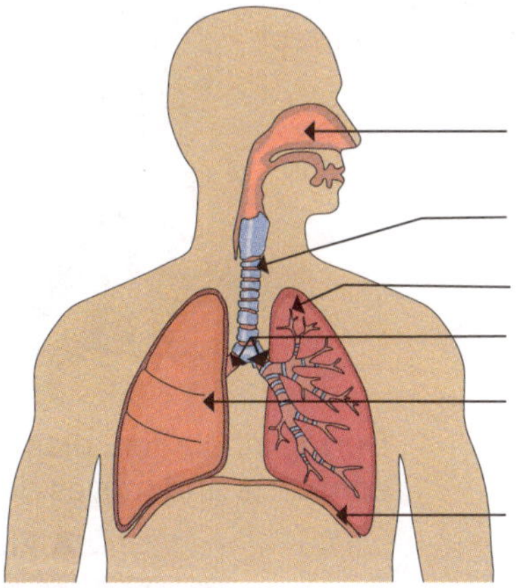

▲ Fig. 4.1 Organs of the respiratory system

A large muscular sheet called **diaphragm** forms the base of the ribcage. The dome-shaped diaphragm separates the stomach and other organs of the digestive system from the chest cavity.

Structure and functions of the parts of the respiratory system

Nose	It has two openings called **nostrils** through which air enters. The hair in the nostrils filter the air which enters and the mucous traps the dust and germs present in the air. This inhaled air further enters regions called **nasal cavity** and **pharynx** that help to moisten and regulate the temperature of air. The pharynx is the pathway for both food and air, the entry of which is regulated by a flap-like structure called the epiglottis.
Trachea	It is a tube-like structure that extends from the larynx to the bronchi. Above the trachea is the **larynx**, which has the **vocal cords** that help us in speech.
Bronchi	The lungs are connected to the trachea through bronchi that further branch into bronchioles, which end with alveoli. Movement of air into the lungs is through the bronchi.
Lungs	The two lungs are present in the chest cavity. They are protected by two outer membranes called the **pleura**. A liquid called pleural fluid is present between these two layers. It makes the expansion and contraction of the lungs smoother during breathing.
Alveoli	These are little air sacs that help in gaseous exchange in the lungs.

Mechanism of Breathing

During inhalation, the diaphragm contracts and moves down. The ribcage moves upwards and outwards (expands). This increases the volume of the chest cavity and reduces the pressure inside it. When the pressure inside the lungs reduces, air from outside rushes into the lungs. During exhalation, the diaphragm relaxes as it moves up and returns to its normal dome shape. The ribcage also returns to its normal position. This reduces the volume of the chest cavity, which in turn increases the pressure inside it. Thus, air is expelled out.

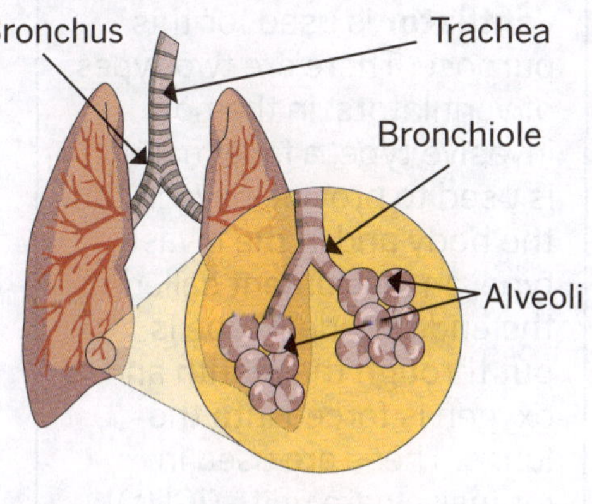

▲ Fig. 4.2 Gaseous exchange occurs in the alveoli

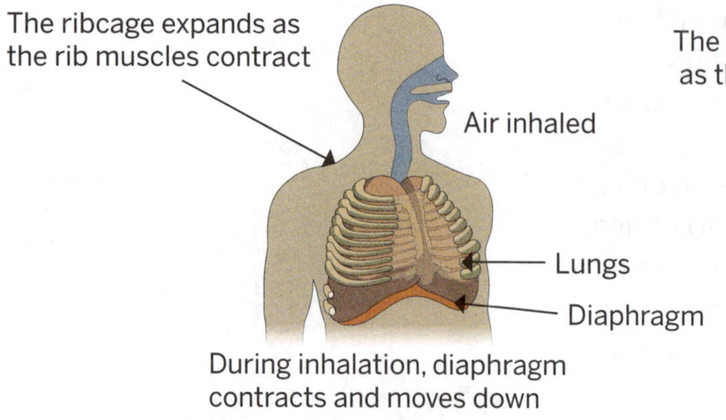

▲ Fig. 4.3 Mechanism of breathing

The number of times a person breathes (inhales and exhales) in a minute is termed as the **breathing rate**. The breathing rate depends on the individual's age and the type of activity he or she carries out. During vigorous exercise or while brisk walking, the breathing rate increases.

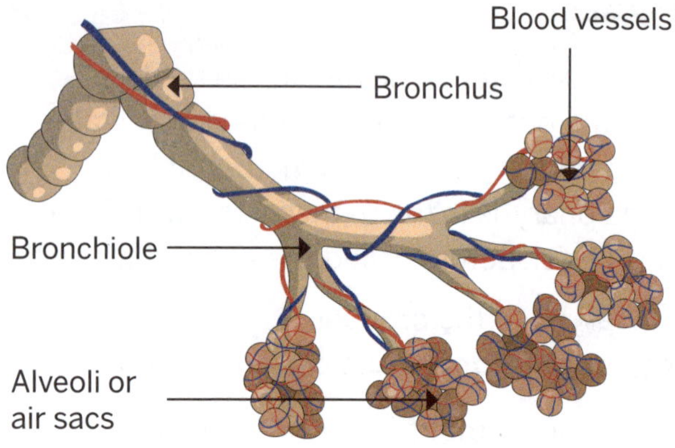

▲ Fig. 4.4 Alveoli and blood vessels

Exchange of Gases (Internal Respiration)

Each alveolus is surrounded by tiny blood vessels called **capillaries**. The exchange of gases takes place between the alveoli of the lungs and the capillaries surrounding it. Each lung contains millions of alveoli, which produce a very large surface area to help in the exchange of gases. While inhaling, the oxygen from the alveoli diffuses into the blood in the capillaries. The carbon dioxide present in the blood also passes out of the blood into the alveoli, which is then exhaled. Alveoli are the structural and functional units of the lungs.

Tech Info

Mechanical ventilation is a technology used in healthcare facilities or hospitals for patients who are unable to breathe in sufficient amounts of oxygen. A machine called **ventilator** is used for this purpose. There are two types of ventilators: in the non-invasive type, a face mask is used to provide oxygen to the body and in the invasive type, an instrument called the endotracheal tube is put through the mouth and oxygen is forced into the lungs. These are used in intensive care units (ICUs).

Cellular Respiration

The oxygen that enters the capillaries from the alveoli passes to the red blood cells (RBCs) of the blood. The RBCs contain a protein called **haemoglobin** that binds with the oxygen and forms a compound called **oxyhaemoglobin**. Oxyhaemoglobin is carried through the blood to all the cells of the body. In the cells, oxygen is released from oxyhaemoglobin. Cells use this oxygen to breakdown glucose (sugar) to form carbon dioxide and water. During this process, energy is released, which is used for the movement of muscles, the growth and repair of cells, bringing about chemical reactions and so on.

The carbon dioxide generated in the cells diffuses into the blood. The blood carries it back to the lungs where it is expelled during exhalation.

Activity

Aim: To prove that exhalation in humans contain carbon dioxide

Materials required: Calcium hydroxide, teaspoon, distilled water, measuring cylinder, 100 mℓ beaker, straw and test tube

Procedure:

1. Pour approximately 20 mℓ of distilled water into the beaker.
2. Add a teaspoon of calcium hydroxide into the water in the beaker and stir well.
3. Leave it closed for some time.
4. Pour the clear liquid into the test tube.
5. Using the straw, blow into the test tube.

Observation: The lime water turns milky.

Conclusion: Milky lime water shows that the exhaled air blown into the lime water contains carbon dioxide. Lime water contains calcium hydroxide and when it is exposed to carbon dioxide, it turns into calcium carbonate. Calcium carbonate is a white salt commonly known as lime.

Common Respiratory Diseases

Respiratory diseases are conditions that affect the respiratory organs. Pathogens, air pollution and smoking are the main causes of respiratory diseases. The major air pollutants that cause respiratory diseases are carbon dioxide, carbon monoxide and suspended particulate matter (SPM). Bronchitis, pneumonia, asthma, common flu and tuberculosis (TB) are the respiratory diseases that commonly occur in human beings.

Bronchitis

It is the infection of bronchial tubes. In this disease, the mucus membranes of the bronchial tubes get inflamed and release more mucus, thus blocking the passage of air. Bronchitis is caused mainly by a viral infection. Other causative agents are air pollution and bacteria.

Symptoms

- Persistent cough with phlegm
- Shortness of breath
- Wheezing
- Fatigue
- Slight fever
- Chest discomfort

Prevention and Treatment

- Use of bronchodilators to increase the passage of air
- Use of cough syrup to reduce cough
- Use of antibiotics in case of bacterial infection

Science in Context

On November 7, 2016, life in New Delhi was paralyzed due to smog. It all happened after the Diwali festival, when the smoke from bursting crackers and fog mixed up to form a dense smog. Due to this people of Delhi suffered from many respiratory disorders.

- Drink plenty of fluids and take rest
- Wash your hands before and after meals and after using the washroom to prevent exposure to pathogens

Pneumonia

Pneumonia is mainly caused by the bacterium *Streptococcus pneumoniae*. It is also caused by other bacterial species and viruses. It results in inflammation of lungs where alveoli are filled with fluids.

Symptoms

- Persistent cough with coloured phlegm (based on severity of disease)
- Fever along with chills
- Stabbing chest pain
- Shortness of breath
- Fatigue
- Headache
- Loss of appetite

Prevention and Treatment

- Vaccination for children and adults as precautionary measure
- Drink plenty of fluids and take rest
- Antibiotics are given to treat bacterial pneumonia

Asthma

Asthma is a disease in which there is inflammation of airways for long period of time. The causative agents are genetic factors and environmental factors such as air pollution, extreme weather conditions and allergens. There is no cure for asthma and the symptoms like inflammation are reduced with the help of medications such as bronchodilators (taken commonly with the help of inhalers).

▲ Fig. 4.5 Inhalers used for treatment of asthma

Symptoms

- Difficulty in breathing
- Chest pain
- Cough
- Wheezing

Prevention and Treatment

- Avoid triggers and irritants that cause asthma
- Bronchodilators and corticosteroids

Tuberculosis (TB)

Tuberculosis is caused by the bacterium *Mycobacterium tuberculosis*. It affects the lungs and spreads to other people through droplet infection. The pathogens are released to air as droplets when infected people cough, spit or sneeze. It widely affects people who smoke and are infected with HIV.

Symptoms

- Cough with blood tinged phlegm
- Fever
- Night sweating
- Chills
- Weight loss and loss of appetite
- Fatigue

Prevention and Treatment

- BCG vaccination to just born infants
- Early diagnostic tests when cough persists for long time
- Infected persons should avoid careless spitting, coughing and sneezing
- Long courses of antibiotics

Keywords

Respiration: the process of breaking down of food into carbon dioxide, water and energy in a living being

Breathing: the process of obtaining oxygen and releasing carbon dioxide in a living being

Trachea: It is also called windpipe; inhaled air enters this tube-like structure from the nasal cavity

Bronchi: Two smaller tubes that branch out from the trachea

Bronchioles: Smaller tubes that branch out from the bronchi inside the lungs

Alveoli: Tiny air sacs at the end of the bronchioles, where the exchange of gases takes place

Ribcage: A cage-like structure made of bones that protect the lungs

Diaphragm: A large muscular sheet that forms the base of the ribcage

Breathing rate: The number of times a person breathes (inhales and exhales) in a minute

Phlegm: A thick viscous substance secreted by the mucous membranes of the respiratory passages

Pathogen: A microorganism that can cause disease

Inflammation: The reaction of tissues to injury orinfection, characterized by heat, redness, swelling and pain

Wheezing: A husky, rasping or whistling sound while breathing

Allergens: Any substance capable of inducing an allergy

Antibiotics: Chemical substances produced by various microorganisms, esp. fungi, that are capable of destroying or inhibiting the growth of microorganisms

Bronchodilators: Any drug or other agent that causes dilation of the bronchial tubes by relaxing bronchial muscles

In a Nutshell

- Respiration is the oxidation of glucose that releases carbon dioxide, water and energy.
- Breathing is a process of inhaling oxygen and exhaling carbon dioxide.
- The organs of the human respiratory system are nasal cavity, trachea, alveoli, bronchi, lungs and diaphragm.
- The inhaled air passes through the nostrils and enters the nasal cavity. From the nasal cavity, the air enters the windpipe (trachea).
- The windpipe branches into two smaller tubes called bronchi (singular: bronchus). Each bronchus enters into a lung.
- In the lungs, each bronchus branches out into smaller tubes called bronchioles. At the end of these tubes, there are tiny air sacs called alveoli (singular: alveolus).
- The walls of the alveoli are lined with a network of blood vessels and capillaries to facilitate the exchange of gases.
- Lungs are present in the chest cavity,enclosed by the ribcage. The diaphragm forms the base of the ribcage.
- The dome-shaped diaphragm separates the stomach and other organs of the digestive system from the chest cavity.
- The RBCs contain a protein called haemoglobin that binds with the oxygen and forms a compound called oxyhaemoglobin. Oxyhaemoglobin is carried through the blood to all the cells of the body.
- In the cells, oxygen is released from oxyhaemoglobin. Cells use this oxygen to breakdown glucose (sugar) to form carbon dioxide and water. During this process, energy is released.
- The carbon dioxide generated in the cells diffuses into the blood. The blood carries it back to the lungs where it is expelled during exhalation.
- There are alveoli in the two lungs in the human body that help in the exchange of gases.

Exercise

1 Choose the correct answer for each of the following.

a. Which of the following is not a part of the human respiratory system?

i. Alveoli ii. Bronchioles
iii. Tracheoles iv. Bronchi

b. During inhalation, the diaphragm moves

i. up
ii. down
iii. both up and down
iv. does not move

c. Blood-tinged phlegm is a symptom of ________.

i. Bronchitis
ii. Asthmatic attack
iii. Tuberculosis
iv. Common cold

2 Fill in the blanks.

a. In human beings, breathing out is also called ________ (inhalation/exhalation).

b. The large muscular sheet that forms the base of the rib cage is called ________ (diaphragm/pleural layer).

c. Pneumonia is caused by bacteria ________. (*Mycobacterium tuberculosis*/*Streptococcus pneumoniae*)

d. In asthmatic attacks, inflammation is reduced using ________. (corticosteroids/progesterone)

3 Write T for True and F for False.

a. Breakdown of glucose in the presence of oxygen in the cells is called external respiration.

b. Carbon dioxide is given out during respiration.

c. The windpipe branches into two smaller tubes called trachea.

d. Gaseous exchange occurs in the alveoli of the lungs.

4 Define the following terms.

a. Respiration b. Breathing
c. Cellular respiration

5 Differentiate between the following.

a. Internal and external respiration
b. Inhalation and exhalation
c. Haemoglobin and oxyhaemoglobin

6 Answer the following questions in one word each.

a. What is the windpipe in humans called?
b. What is the causative organism for pneumonia?
c. Name the vaccine given to prevent tuberculosis.

7 Answer the following questions in brief.

a. Write the functions of alveoli.
b. What is the role of diaphragm in the breathing process?
c. Name the vaccine used for tuberculosis in just-born infants.
d. Write the causative agents of bronchitis.

8 Answer the following questions in detail.

a. Explain the mechanism of breathing in human beings.
b. Explain the role of the organs of the human respiratory system.
c. Explain the symptoms and treatment of pneumonia.

9 Think and answer.

Why do we choke and cough sometimes when we swallow food?

(Hint: The epiglottis prevents food and water from entering into the trachea.)

10 Project

Make a model to demonstrate the working of human lungs and diaphragm.

Materials required: A soda or a plastic bottle, a cutter, a Y-shaped tube, a rubber sheet, a string, balloons

Procedure:

1. Drill a hole in the lid/cap of a soda plastic bottle.
2. Make sure that the hole is just as big as the diameter of the Y-shaped tube.
3. Cut the base of the bottle using the cutter and close the lid of the bottle.
4. Fit the Y-shaped tube through the bottom hole into the lid of the bottle.
5. Fix the balloons to each of the arms of the Y-shaped tube through the open base of the bottle.
6. Tie them with rubber bands or strings, so that they are held tightly.
7. Fix a rubber sheet to the bottom of the bottle and tie it with a string or a rubber band to make sure that it is held tightly.
8. Pull and push the rubber sheet to observe the inflation and deflation of the balloons.
9. The balloons are compared to the lungs, the rubber tube to the diaphragm, the Y-shaped tube to trachea and the bronchi.

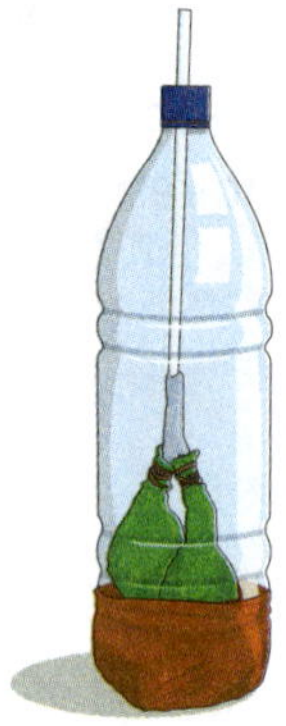

11 In the Library

Refer library books and make a report on diseases of the lungs like bronchitis, asthma and other respiratory disorders.

Worksheet

1. **Draw the arrows to show the direction or air and movement of muscles during breathing.**

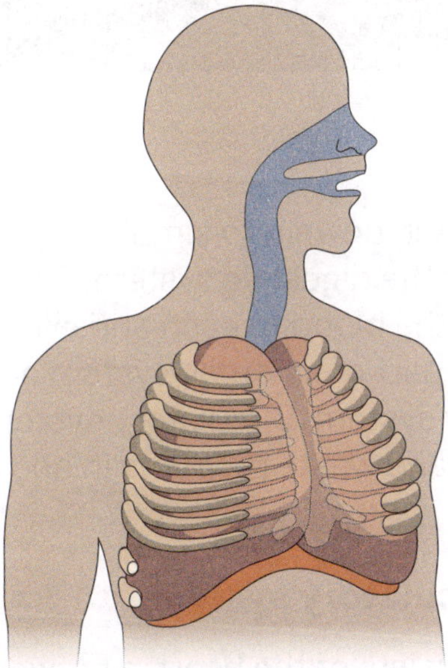

Inhalation

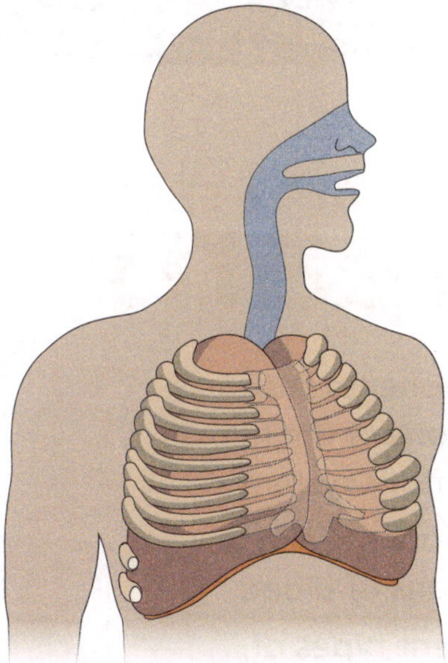

Exhalation

2. **Life Skills**

Have you heard about *mouth-to-mouth resuscitation*? It is an emergency procedure that is done to save a person who has collapsed and stopped breathing. The rescuer blows in air into the mouth of a person who has collapsed. This helps to restore the supply of oxygen. Find out how and learn how it is done and who knows, you might be able to save someone's life some time!

List the steps for the procedure in the space given below:

Human Body: Circulatory System

5

What I shall learn

- Components and functions of the human circulatory system
- Components and functions of blood
- Different types of blood groups
- Blood pressure, heart rate and pulse

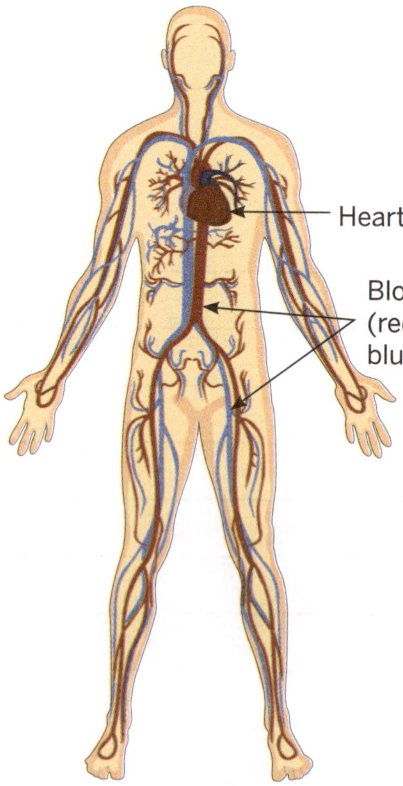

▲ Fig. 5.1 Human circulatory system

Introduction

The food consumed is broken down into simpler substances like glucose by the digestive system. These substances are carried by the blood to each and every cell of the body. The blood is a part of an organ system of the body called the circulatory system. Circulatory system also carries oxygen, water and waste products in and out of the body, respectively.

Components of the circulatory system

The circulatory system consists of the heart, a network of blood vessels and blood.

Heart: The heart is a muscular organ which pumps blood into the larger blood vessels that branch into smaller ones to reach all the parts of a human body. It also receives blood from all the parts of the body.

Blood vessels: These are thin tube-like structures which start from the heart and run through the entire body forming a network. They carry blood from the heart to all the parts of the body, and from different parts of the body back to the heart. The blood vessels are of three types—arteries, veins and capillaries.

Arteries carry blood from the heart to the different parts of the body.

Veins carry blood from different parts of the body to the heart.

Arteries branch out into smaller and thinner blood vessels called arterioles. These further branch into even smaller blood vessels called **capillaries**. Capillaries are the smallest blood vessels. Many capillaries reunite to form veins. Capillaries help in the exchange of gases, water and nutrients between the blood and tissues.

Blood: Blood is a red-coloured fluid that flows through the blood vessels from the heart to all the parts of the body and then back to the heart. It transports the nutrients absorbed from the food, oxygen, carbon dioxide and water inside the body. It also transports the waste products produced in the body to the excretory system so that they can be removed from the body.

Blood- components, functions and blood groups

Blood

Blood consists of a pale yellow liquid called **plasma** and three types of cells: **red blood cells** (RBCs), **white blood cells** (WBCs) and blood **platelets**. Blood cells are made inside the bone marrow. Each component of blood has a specific function to perform.

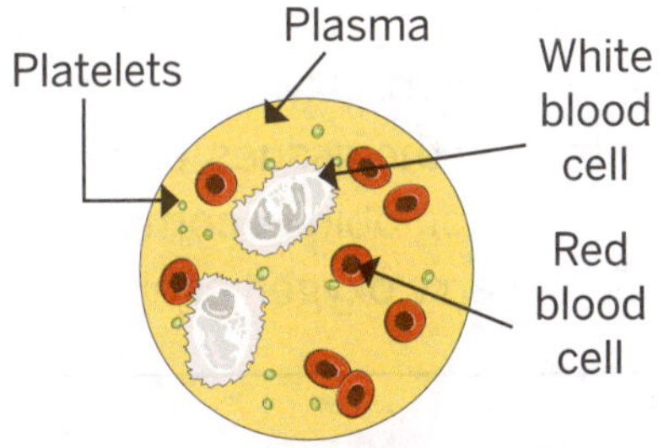

▲ Fig. 5.2 Components of blood

Plasma

- The blood cells are suspended in plasma, which is a yellow-coloured fluid.
- About 90 per cent of plasma is made up of **water**.
- It contains **nutrients** like glucose, amino acids, proteins and hormones and excretory products like carbon dioxide, salts and fat molecules.
- It carries nutrients and oxygen to every cell of the body and transports the waste products from the cells to the excretory system.
- It also contains **antibodies** (proteins produced by the body that protect us against pathogens) and **fibrinogen** (a protein that helps in clotting of blood).

Red Blood Cells (RBCs) or Erythrocytes

- In Latin, *erythro* means red and *cyte* means cell.
- They are biconcave or disc-shaped cells.
- They are produced in the bone marrow. Every RBC has a lifespan ranging from 100 to 120 days.
- They lose their nucleus when they mature.
- They are red in colour due to the presence of the pigment called **haemoglobin**, which helps to carry oxygen to every cell in the body.

White Blood Cells (WBCs) or Leucocytes

- In Latin, *leuco* means colourless and *cyte* means cell.
- White blood cells are larger than RBCs. They are colourless and have a nucleus.
- Their main function is to provide immunity against infections by fighting and killing germs.

Know the Scientist

William Harvey (1578–1657), an English physician, was the first to describe the circulation of blood to the brain and various parts of the body by the heart and the properties of blood.

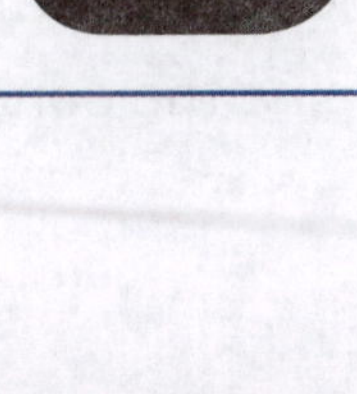

Science in Context

Oxygen combines with haemoglobin in the red blood cells to form **oxyhaemoglobin**. When blood reaches the cells and tissues of the body that need oxygen, oxyhaemoglobin breaks down into oxygen and haemoglobin. Oxygen is then utilized by the tissues, and the haemoglobin becomes free to carry oxygen again.

Do You Know?

The debris of white blood cells killed while battling pathogens or foreign bodies come out of the body as a yellow coloured fluid called **pus**.

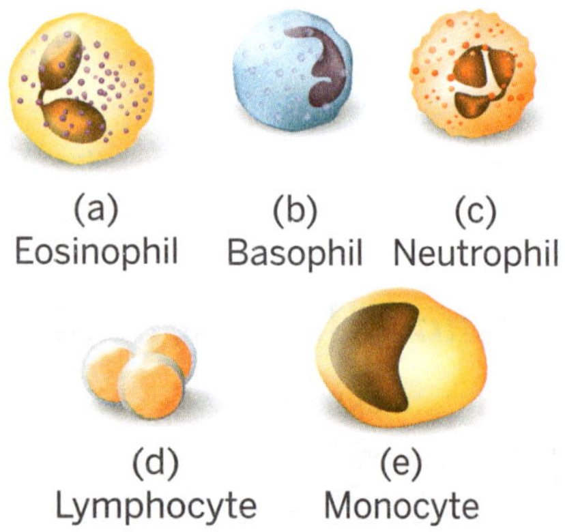

▲ Fig. 5.3 Different types of WBCs

- They do not have a fixed shape; they keep changing their shape constantly. This enables them to easily reach the site of infection. They also secrete antibodies for protection against diseases.
- The life span of WBCs range from a few hours to two weeks.
- WBCs are of two types:
  a. **Granulocytes**: They have granules in their cytoplasm. They are of three types:
    i. **Neutrophils**: Their nucleus has three lobes. They account for 30–70 per cent of WBCs.
    ii. **Basophils**: Their nucleus is not distinctly lobed. They account for 0.5 per cent of WBCs.
    iii. **Eosinophils**: Their nucleus is two-lobed. They account for 2–5 per cent of WBCs.
  b. **Agranulocytes**: They do not have granules in the cytoplasm. They are of two types:
    i. **Lymphocytes**: Their nucleus is large and spherical. They account for 25 per cent of WBCs.
    ii. **Monocytes**: Their nucleus is large and shaped like a horse shoe. They account for 3–8 per cent of WBCs.

Platelets or Thrombocytes

- In Latin, *thrombo* means to clot and *cyte* means cell.
- They are smaller than RBCs. They do not have a nucleus, and are colourless.
- They are irregular in shape.
- They help in clotting of blood during injuries and prevent loss of blood.
- Their life span ranges from 8 to 14 days.

The blood cells are destroyed in the liver once their lifespan is complete. The components are reused to form new cells.

Functions of Blood

The main functions of blood are as follows:

- Transports oxygen and nutrients to all the cells and tissues of the body.
- Transports waste products generated in the body like carbon dioxide and urea to excretory organs for removal.
- Carries hormones and enzymes from the secretory glands to the site of action.
- Carries antibodies and the clotting protein called fibrinogen.
- Regulates body temperature by controlling the amount of water in the body and maintains the body temperature.
- Maintains the concentration of chemical substances in the tissues and cells.

Activity 1

Aim: To view the red blood cells (RBCs) and white blood cells (WBCs) under the microscope

Materials required: Microscope, permanent slides of RBC and WBC

Procedure: Focus the permanent slides of RBC and WBC under the high-power objective of the microscope, with the help of your teacher.

Observation: Observe the slides under the microscope and complete the observation table below:

Structures observed	White blood cells	Red blood cells
Nucleus		
Shape of the cell		
Size of the cell		

Blood Groups

The surface of red blood cells has substances called **antigens**, which are made up of inherited proteins.

Based on the type of antigens, human blood can be grouped into the following types:

Blood group A: having antigen A

Blood group B: having antigen B

Blood group AB: having both antigen A and antigen B

Blood group O: having neither antigen A nor antigen B

Rh Blood Grouping System

Other than antigens A and B, the red blood cells have an antigen known as the Rh antigen. This antigen was first discovered in the rhesus monkey (*Rhesus macaque*). If the Rh factor or antigen is present on the RBCs, the blood group is called + (positive) and in the absence of Rh antigen or factor, the blood group is called – (negative).

Science in Context

Erythroblastosis fetalis is a condition that occurs when the mother's blood group is incompatible with the baby in her womb. The incompatibility of their antigens triggers an immune response against the baby's red blood cells. This destroys the baby's blood cells and the baby may suffer from severe anaemia (deficiency in RBCs), and the condition may be fatal.

Do You Know?

There is a rare blood group called the Bombay blood group. It is named after the place where the first person discovered to have this blood grouped belonged.

A person with the Bombay blood group lacks any type of antigens and produces antibodies against the A, B, O and Rh antigens, thus becoming incompatible with any of the normal blood groups. It occurs once in a million and is rarely found in blood banks.

Revision Zone

Write T for True and F for False.

1. Blood is made up of only one type of cell called red blood cell.
2. Platelet cells in blood are also called thrombocytes.
3. The nucleus of neutrophils has two lobes.
4. A person with blood group AB has both antigen A and antigen B on the surface of RBCs.
5. Blood helps in maintaining the body temperature.

Blood Vessels

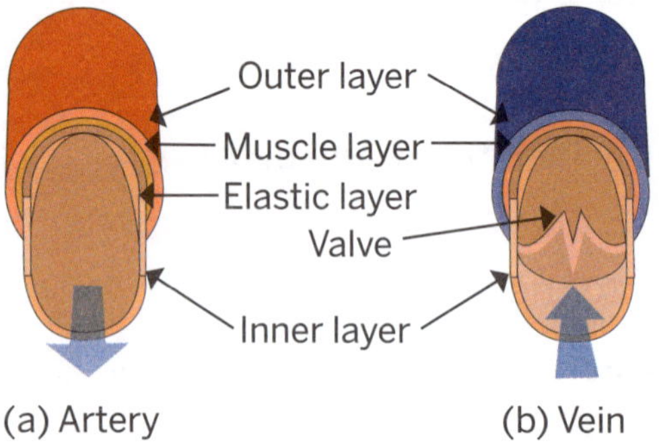

▲ Fig. 5.4 Structure of artery and vein

The blood in our body moves through tube-like structures called **blood vessels**. Blood vessels are of three types: arteries, veins and capillaries.

Arteries: Arteries transport blood from the heart to the organs. They generally carry **oxygenated** blood (blood rich in oxygen), except the pulmonary artery, which carries deoxygenated blood from the heart to the lungs. They have thick elastic walls as blood flows through them with high pressure.

Veins: Veins bring blood to the heart from all parts of the body. They generally carry deoxygenated blood, except the pulmonary vein, which brings oxygenated blood from the lungs to the heart. Veins have thinner walls than arteries.

Veins have **valves**, structures that prevent the blood from flowing back to the organs. Veins lie closer to the skin surface and can be seen as greenish-blue lines in our hands and legs.

Capillaries: When an artery reaches an organ, it splits into smaller arteries called **arterioles**, which further split to form a network of extremely thin blood vessels called **capillaries**. The capillaries join together to form small veins called **venules**, which ultimately join to form veins.

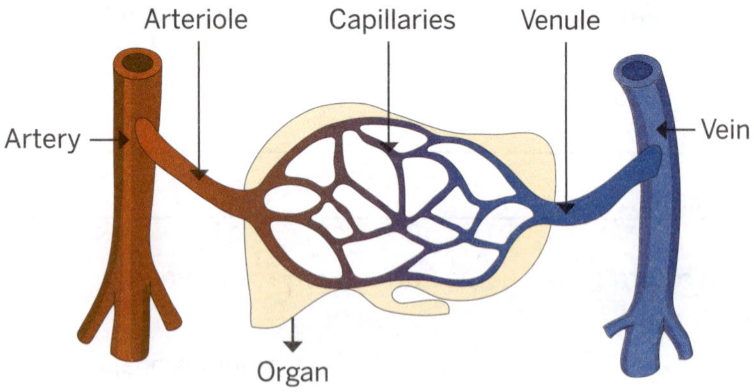

▲ Fig. 5.5 A network of capillaries

Exchange of materials such as nutrients, chemical substances and gases between the blood and the cells occurs in the capillaries.

The blood pressure in the capillaries is lower than that in the arteries but higher than that in the veins.

A comparison between the three blood vessels

	Artery	Capillary	Vein
Function	Carries oxygenated blood from heart to other parts of the body at high blood pressure	Transports nutrients and other substances to every cell and carries back the waste products and other substances	Carries deoxygenated blood from different parts of the body to the heart at low blood pressure
Structure of wall	Thick wall with elastic and muscle tissues	Very thin wall	Thin wall with less elastic and muscle tissues than arteries
Hollow cavity	Narrow	Very narrow	Wide
Valves	Absent	Absent	Present

Human Heart

The heart is a fist-sized muscular organ found in the chest cavity towards the left lung. It pumps blood to all parts of the body. It beats 60–80 times a minute throughout our life.

The heart is enclosed in a double-layered sac called **pericardium**, which is filled with a fluid called **pericardial fluid**. This fluid protects the heart from jerks and shocks during contraction and relaxation.

> **Remember**
> All the arteries carry oxygenated blood, except for the pulmonary artery, and all the veins carry deoxygenated blood, except for the pulmonary vein.

Structure of the Heart

The heart is made up of four chambers. The upper left and right chambers are the **atria** (singular: **atrium**, also called **auricle**), and the lower left and right chambers are the **ventricles**. The atria and ventricles are separated from each other by walls or partitions, which have **valves** in them. Valves allow the blood to flow only in one direction.

There are four valves in the heart:

1. **Tricuspid valve**: This valve is between right atrium and right ventricle.
2. **Pulmonic valve**: This valve is between right ventricle and pulmonary artery.
3. **Mitral or bicuspid valve**: This valve is between left atrium and left ventricle.
4. **Aortic valve**: This valve is between left ventricle and the aorta.

The right auricle opens into the right ventricle and the left auricle into the left ventricle. Consequently, the blood on the right side of the heart remains completely separated from the blood on the left side of the heart.

Blood rich in carbon dioxide flows through the right side of the heart, while the blood rich in oxygen flows through the left side of the heart. A partition called **septum** separates the left side of the heart from the right, preventing the mixing of oxygenated blood with deoxygenated blood. The arteries and veins in the heart connect to the other parts of the body. The major blood vessels that originate in the heart are:

Vena cava: It is a large vein that collects blood rich in carbon dioxide from all parts of the body through other smaller veins and empties the blood into the right atrium. (This blood then goes to the right ventricle.)

Pulmonary artery: It carries blood rich in carbon dioxide from the right ventricle of the heart to the lungs. (In the lungs the carbon dioxide is removed from the blood and oxygen is taken up into the blood.)

Pulmonary vein: It brings back oxygenated blood from the lungs to the left atrium of the heart. (From the left atrium the blood comes to the left ventricle.)

Aorta: It is the largest artery that receives blood rich in oxygen from the left ventricle. This oxygenated blood is then circulated to different parts of the body.

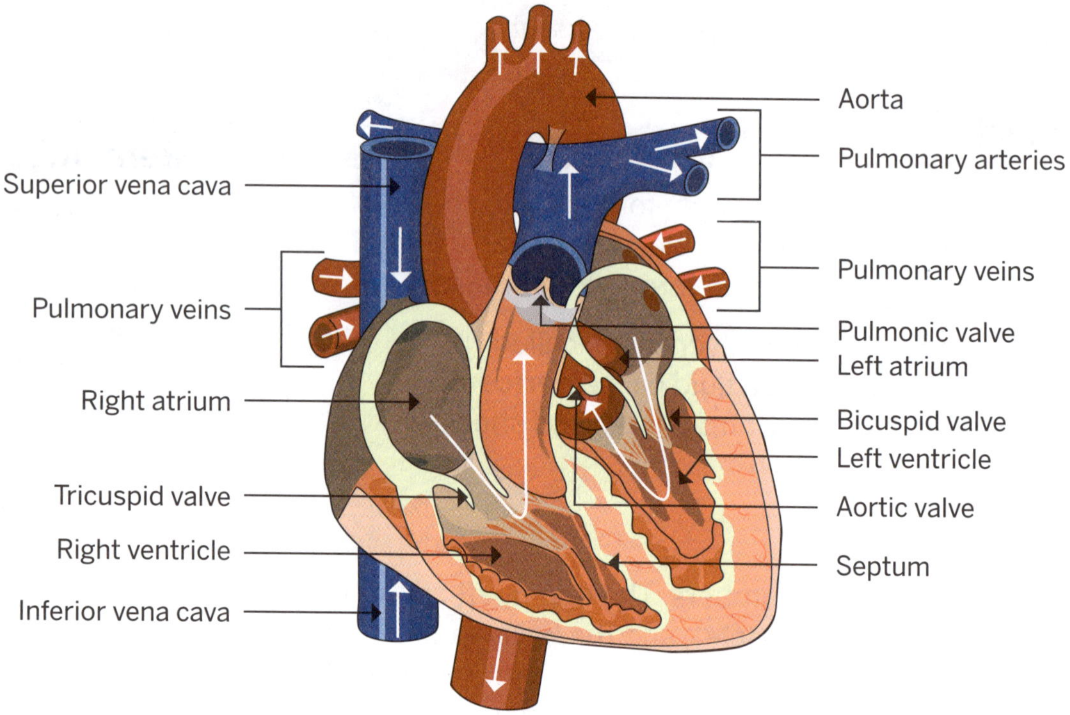

▲ Fig. 5.6 Structure of the human heart

Circulation of Blood

The movement of deoxygenated blood away from the heart to the lungs and the movement of oxygenated blood from the lungs to the heart is known as **pulmonary circulation**.

The vena cava carries deoxygenated blood to the right atrium. Once the right atrium is filled with deoxygenated blood, it contracts. This contraction pushes the blood through the one-way tricuspid valve into the right ventricle.

When the blood fills the right ventricle, it contracts, pumping blood through the pulmonary artery and to the lungs. The capillaries in the lungs exchange the deoxygenated blood (rich in carbon dioxide) with the oxygenated blood (rich in oxygen). The oxygenated blood is carried by the pulmonary veins to the left atrium of the heart.

Do You Know?

The study of blood flow is called **haemodynamics**.

When blood fills the left atrium, it contracts. This pushes blood to the one-way bicuspid or mitral valve into the left ventricle. The left ventricle pumps the oxygenated blood through the aorta to the different parts of the body away from the heart.

The movement of blood from the heart to the other body parts, except lungs, and back to the heart is known as **systemic circulation**. The aorta carries oxygenated blood to a network of capillaries, which transport blood to every cell in the body. The deoxygenated blood is received back or exchanged by the capillaries, and then collected by the venules and passed to the veins. The veins carry the deoxygenated blood back to the heart. There are two main veins in the body. The superior vena cava is the major vein that brings deoxygenated blood from the upper parts of the body to the heart. The inferior vena cava is the vein that brings deoxygenated blood from the lower parts of the body to the heart.

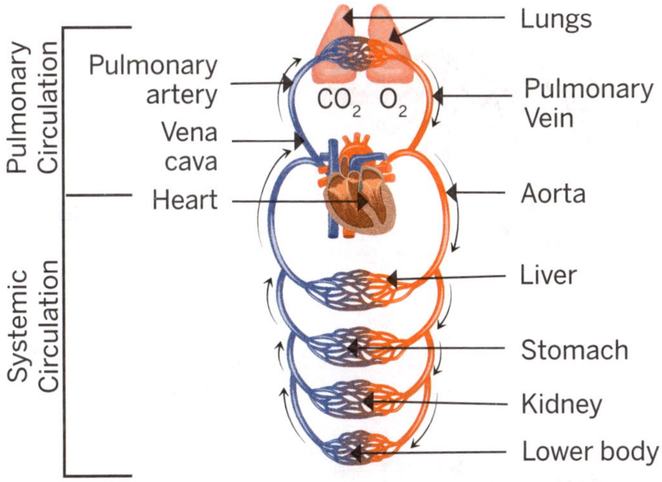

▲ Fig. 5.7 Double circulation

Pulmonary and systemic circulation allow the blood to flow twice through the heart. This is known as **double circulation**.

Cardiac Cycle

The phase when the cardiac muscles relax and allow the chambers of the heart to get filled with blood is known as **diastole**. During diastole, the deoxygenated blood from the body enters the heart. The phase when the cardiac muscles contract and pump blood to the other parts is known as **systole**. During systole, oxygenated blood from the heart circulates to the body. One diastole and systole make a complete **cardiac cycle**. A cardiac cycle is commonly called a **heartbeat**.

Blood Pressure

The wall of the blood vessels experiences pressure due to the force of the flowing blood. This pressure is called **blood pressure**. The pressure is high when the heart contracts and is known as **systolic pressure**. The pressure is low when the heart relaxes and is known as **diastolic pressure**.

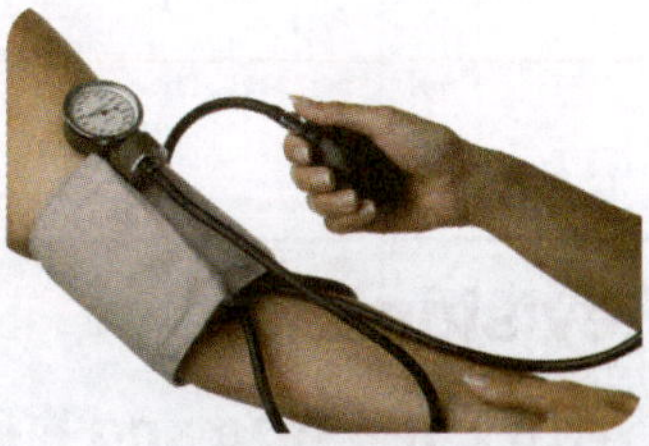
▲ Fig. 5.8 Sphygmomanometer

Blood pressure (BP) of a person is calculated by taking the systolic pressure over diastolic pressure. A healthy adult should have a blood pressure measuring about 120/80. However, the BP varies according to the gender, age and the health condition of the person.

Sphygmomanometer is the instrument used to measure blood pressure.

Heart Rate and Pulse

The number of times the heart beats or the rate at which the heart beats in one minute is known as **heart rate**. **Stethoscope** is the instrument used to measure heart rate.

▲ Fig. 5.9 Stethoscope

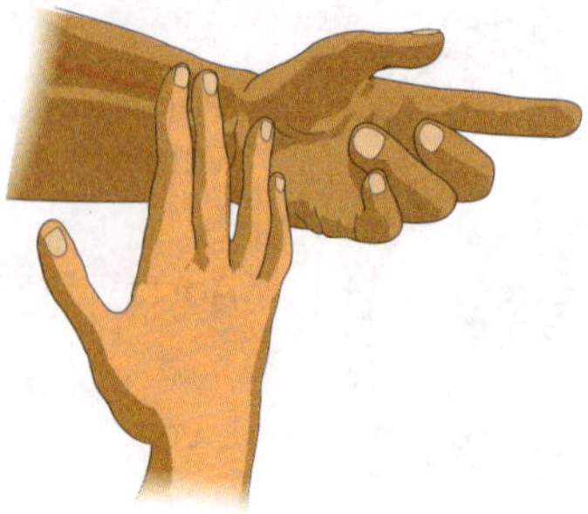

▲ Fig. 5.10 Checking pulse

With every heartbeat, ventricles contract and push the blood into the arteries. This results in a jerk like motion which generates a wave of pressure in the arteries. This wave of pressure is called **pulse**. The pulse rate in a healthy adult is 70-75 per minute. But it varies according to age, gender and occupation. The pulse rate increases after exercise.

The arteries in the wrist, near the elbow and in the neck run very close to the skin. Pulse can be felt in these points. By placing the index and middle finger gently and firmly in these places, we can feel our pulse.

Activity 2

Aim: To count the pulse before and after exercise

Procedure: Divide the entire class into groups of two members, A and B.

1. Ask student A of each group to count and record the pulse rate of student B in the table given below.
2. Ask the student B to squat 10 times or exercise for few minutes.
3. Ask student A to count student B's pulse after squatting and record the pulse rate.
4. Repeat the same procedures for student A with student B recording the pulse rate.

Observation:

Observation	Pulse rate before exercise	Pulse rate after exercise
Student A		
Student B		

Conclusion: The pulse rate increases after exercise.

Revision Zone

Write T for True and F for False.

1. Heart rate is measured using a sphygmomanometer.
2. Blood pressure consists of only the systolic pressure.

Healthy Heart

Heart is an organ that works continuously throughout the lifetime of an individual. Therefore, keeping the heart healthy is necessary to keep the body healthy. Today most of the cardio-vascular diseases occur due to improper diet and lack of exercise.

The food items that are good for heart are:

- Fish such as salmon and tuna that are rich in omega 3-fatty acids
- Nuts such as walnuts and almonds
- Dark chocolate
- Low -fat or fat-free dairy products
- Oatmeal
- Fruits rich in beta-carotene, potassium and fiber
- Flax seeds are also rich in omega-3 fatty acids

Exercising regularly makes our body fit and healthy. Exercises in the forms of walking, running, jogging and stretching can be done to keep the heart healthy. Doing these exercises regularly burns calories, lowers the blood pressure and reduces the bad cholesterol (disrupts the function of heart) in your body.

Keywords

Plasma: fluid part of the blood made up of 90 per cent water

Erythrocytes: red blood cells

Haemoglobin: the red-coloured pigment in blood

Leucocytes: white blood cells

Antibody: a protein complex produced by the body to destroy a foreign substance or pathogens

Rh antigen: antigen present in blood

Stethoscope: an instrument used to measure heart beat

Sphygmomanometer: an instrument used to measure blood pressure

In a Nutshell

- The circulatory system consists of heart, blood and blood vessels.
- Blood acts like a medium of transportation in the circulatory system.
- The fluid part of the blood that is made up of about 90 per cent of water is called plasma.
- Red blood cells or RBCs, white blood cells or WBCs and platelets are suspended in plasma.
- Depending on the antigens present on the surface of RBCs, there are four types of blood groups, namely, A, B, AB and O.
- Rh factor further groups blood into positive and negative blood types.
- When blood is transfused from one person to another, the RBC antigens should match.
- Incompatible blood types lump together and clog the blood vessels in the body obstructing the circulation of blood. This is known as agglutination.
- The heart is a pumping organ that has four chambers: two auricles and two ventricles.
- Pulmonary and systemic circulation allow the blood to flow twice through the blood vessels. This is known as double circulation.
- Lymph is the tissue fluid that seeps through thin walls of capillaries, and is collected by lymphatic vessels.

Mind Map

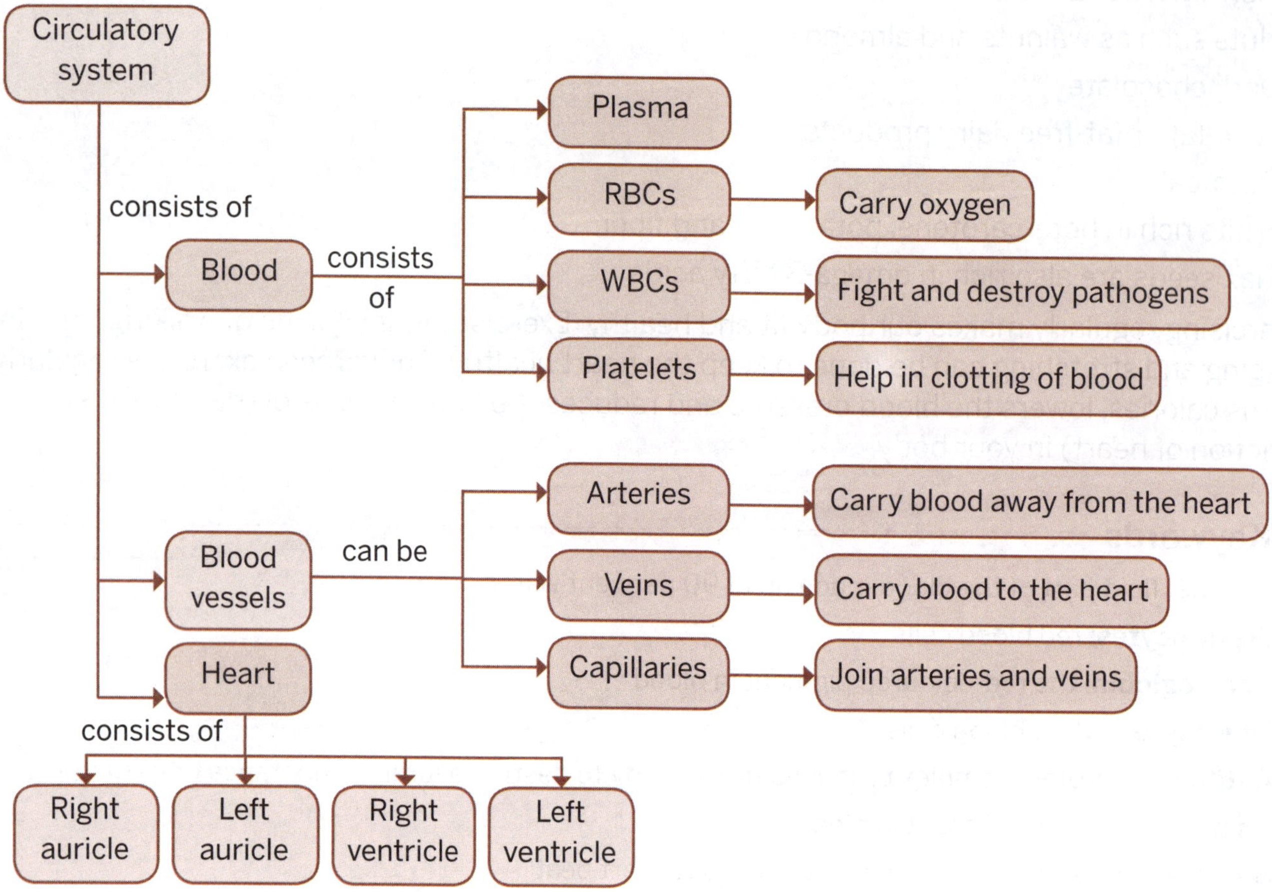
Circulatory system
consists of
Blood
consists of
Plasma
RBCs
Carry oxygen
WBCs
Fight and destroy pathogens
Platelets
Help in clotting of blood
Blood vessels
can be
Arteries
Carry blood away from the heart
Veins
Carry blood to the heart
Capillaries
Join arteries and veins
Heart
consists of
Right auricle
Left auricle
Right ventricle
Left ventricle

Exercise

1 Choose the correct answer for each of the following.

a. Which is the largest artery in the body?
   i. Inferior vena cava
   ii. Pulmonary vein
   iii. Superior vena cava
   iv. Aorta

b. Which of these blood groups is known as universal donor?
   i. A
   ii. B
   iii. AB
   iv. O

c. Which of these blood vessels carries oxygenated blood?
   i. superior vena cava
   ii. inferior vena cava
   iii. pulmonary vein
   iv. None of these

d. Erythrocytes are red in colour due to the presence of
   i. haemoglobin
   ii. nitrogen
   iii. oxygen
   iv. platelets

e. The blood vessel that carries deoxygenated blood from different parts of the body to the heart is
   i. aorta
   ii. vein
   iii. artery
   iv. capillary

f. Which of these instruments is used to measure heartbeat?
   i. Sphygmomanometer
   ii. Microscope
   iii. Stethoscope
   iv. Thermometer

g. Which of the following components of blood helps it to clot?
   i. Erythrocyte
   ii. Monocyte
   iii. Lymphocyte
   iv. Platelet

h. In the blood type AB. the antigens present are
   i. A and B
   ii. only A
   iii. only B
   iv. neither A nor B

i. Which of the following is a source of omega-3 fatty acids?
   I. Fruits
   II. Dairy products
   III. Dark chocolate
   IV. Flax seeds

2 Fill in the blanks.

a. Haemoglobin is __________ (a pigment/an antibody) found in the blood.

b. The right side of the heart has __________ (oxygenated/ deoxygenated) blood.

c. Veins have __________ (thicker/ thinner) walls than arteries.

d. The protein called fibrinogen helps blood to __________ (flow freely/clot).

e. The upper two chambers of heart are called __________ (auricle/ventricle).

f. The __________ (red/white) blood cells fight and destroy pathogens.

g. Blood is taken away from the heart by __________ (arteries/veins).

3 Write T for True and F for False.

a. Sphygmomanometer is used to measure heartbeat.

b. Blood platelets are also called thrombocytes.

c. The force of blood against blood vessels creates blood pressure.

d. Blood pressure is high when the heart contracts.

e. Arteries connect veins to capillaries.

f. Human heart is four-chambered.

4 Define the following.

a. Circulatory system
b. Plasma
c. Rh factor
d. Erythrocytes
e. Pulse

5 Differentiate between the following.

a. Arteries and veins
b. Erythrocytes and leucocytes
c. Heart rate and pulse
d. Pulmonary circulation and systemic circulation
e. Systolic pressure and diastolic pressure

6 Choose the odd one out. Give reasons for your choice.

a. Heart, veins, blood, kidney
b. Plasma, WBC, valve, RBC
c. Oxygen, carbon dioxide, haemoglobin, lymph
d. Neutrophils, haemoglobin, basophils, eosinophils
e. A, B, AB, Rh

7 Give reasons for the following.

a. The oxygenated and deoxygenated blood in the heart do not get mixed.
b. Blood pressure is lower in veins than in arteries.

8 Answer the following questions in brief.

a. What is circulatory system?
b. What are the functions of the circulatory system?
c. What are the different blood groups in human beings? What is the basis of grouping them?
d. Write a short note on systemic circulation.
e. Write a short note on pulmonary circulation.
f. What happens to the blood that comes to the right ventricle?

9 Answer the following questions in detail.

a. List the functions of blood in our body.
b. Describe the components of blood.
c. Describe the different types of white blood cells.
d. Explain the structure of the human heart.
e. The circulatory system in humans is known as double circulatory system. Explain.
f. Explain the healthy diet and exercise to be followed to maintain a healthy heart.

10 Think and answer.

a. The left ventricle of the heart has thicker walls than the right ventricle. Why? (Hint: Ventricles pump blood to the different parts of body.)
b. Precautions must be taken before transfusion of blood even when the blood type matches. Explain.
(Hint: Blood is a liquid medium which also carries various germs.)

11 Project

a. Visit a nearby blood bank and learn more about blood groups and blood transfusions. Make a report.
b. Visit a nearby pathology lab to find out how blood groups can be detected. Also learn how blood is tested to reveal infections.

12 In the Laboratory

Observe a model of the heart and the circulatory system in the laboratory.

13 In the Library

a. Collect information about heart-lung bypass machine and how it helps to operate on the heart during open heart surgeries.
b. Maintaining a healthy lifestyle keeps the heart healthy. Avoid junk food and excess salt, exercise regularly and maintain an appropriate weight for your height and age. Find out more about other activities that can be done to keep the heart healthy.

Worksheet

1. **Identify the blood cells shown below and write their names in the space provided.**

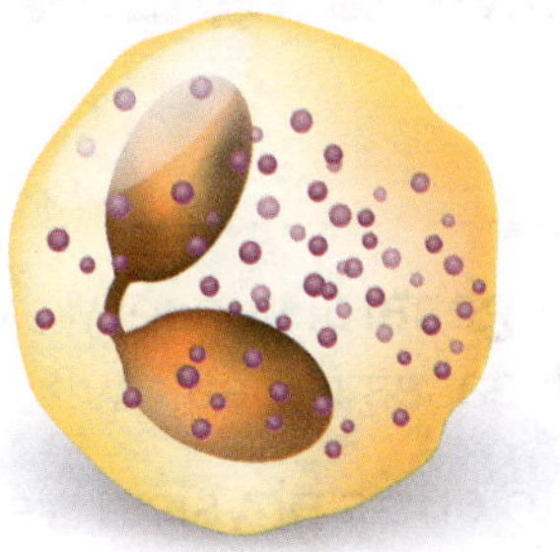

____

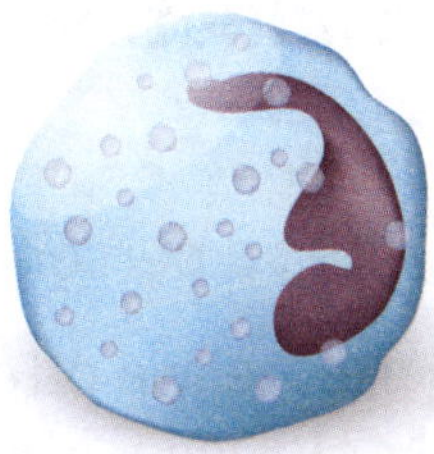

____

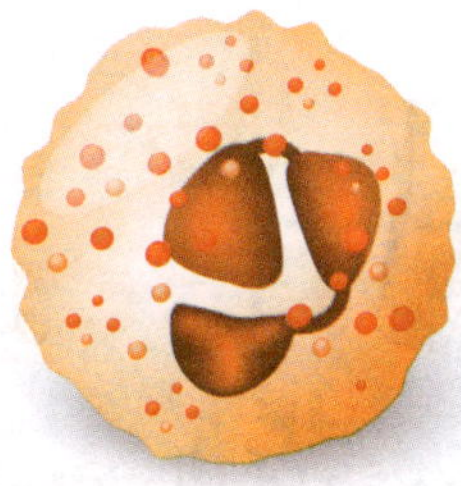

____

____

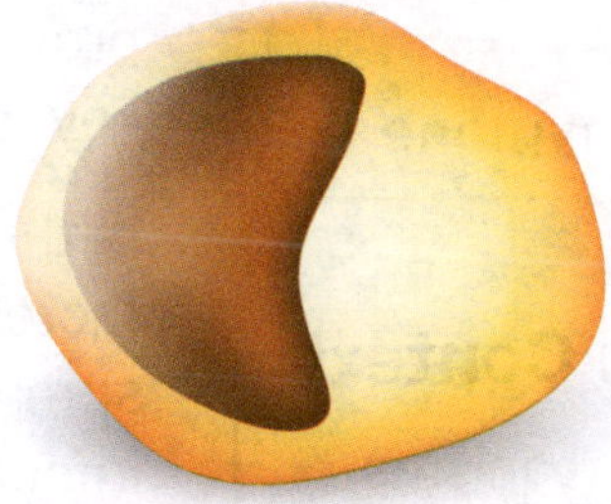

____

2. **Life Skills**

Heart disease has become common nowadays due to the unhealthy lifestyle followed by people. People who exercise regularly, eat a healthy diet that consists of low-fat foods and consume more vegetables and fruits can reduce the risk of heart diseases. You can also advise people who have heart disease to take the following precautionary measures:

a. Quitting smoking drops the risk of heart disease dramatically.

b. Doing at least 30–60 minutes of moderate physical activity most days of the week helps one to remain healthy. Activities such as gardening, taking the stairs instead of an elevator and walking are moderate physical activities.

c. Keeping a check on one's body mass index (BMI) and maintain a healthy weight according to one's height.

Find out and list three more measures to reduce the risk of heart disease.

____

____

____

Health and Hygiene

6

What I shall learn

- Types of diseases
- Spreading of diseases
- Prevention of infection
- Personal hygiene
- Community hygiene

Science in Context

Not all microorganisms are harmful. Some are also beneficial for us. For example, the bacterium *E. coli* lives in the intestine of human beings. It obtains the nutrients for its growth from the intestine, In return, it helps in the digestion of food.

Remember

Disease is a pathological condition of a body part, an organ or a system resulting from various causes such as infection, genetic defect or environmental stress and is characterized by an identifiable group of signs or symptoms.
– World Health Organization (WHO)

Introduction

What does 'being healthy' mean? In a general sense, we often say that a person who is free from diseases is healthy.

Therefore, we often attribute health to one's physical wellbeing only. However, the true meaning of health is not the absence of diseases but also mental and social well-being.

Good nutrition, personal hygiene, cleanliness of surroundings, protection from diseases and regular exercise are some of the key factors necessary to live a healthy life.

In this chapter, we will discuss about these factors in detail, and learn how diseases spread and ways to prevent and avoid infection.

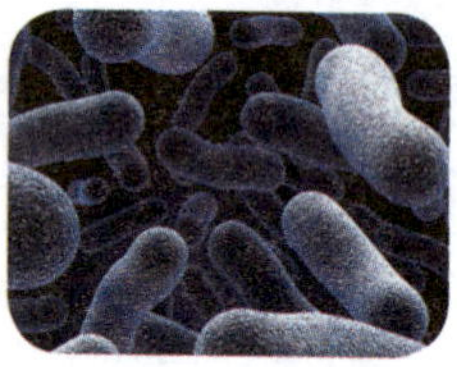

▲ Fig. 6.1 Bacteria

Types of Diseases

On the basis of how they spread, diseases can be categorized into two types: communicable and non-communicable diseases.

▲ Fig. 6.2 Fungi

Diseases that cannot spread from one person to another are called **non-communicable diseases**. These diseases are caused by lack of or excess of nutrients in the body or the malfunctioning of organs.

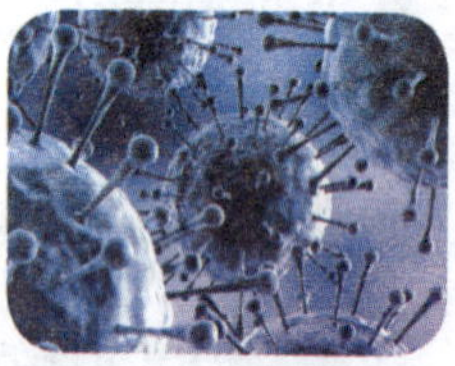

▲ Fig. 6.3 Virus

Diseases that can spread from one person to another are called **communicable diseases** (Table 6.1). These diseases are caused by harmful microorganisms like bacteria, viruses, fungi and protozoa. Microorganisms that cause diseases are called **pathogens** or **germs**.

▲ Fig. 6.4 Protozoan

Table 6.1 Some communicable diseases

Disease	Pathogen	Spreads through
Cholera	Bacteria – *Vibrio cholerae*	Contaminated food and water
Typhoid	Bacteria – *Salmonella typhi*	Contaminated food and water, and flies
Tuberculosis	Bacteria – *Mycobacterium tuberculosis*	Air, spit of the patients and dust
Chickenpox	Virus – *Varicella zoster*	Air during initial days, then contact with blisters
Influenza (Flu)	Virus – *Influenza virus*	Air
Rabies	Virus – *Rabies virus*	Bite of a rabid dog and other animals
Diarrhoea	Bacteria – *E. coli, Salmonella, Shigella* (It is important to note here that there are many types of *E. coli* and most of them are harmless, while there are a few types that cause diarrhoea.) Virus – *Rotavirus, Hepatitis viruses* Protozoa – *Entamoeba*	Contaminated food and water
Malaria	Protozoa – *Plasmodium*	Bite of female *Anopheles* mosquito

How Communicable Diseases Spread

Communicable diseases can spread through the following modes.

Diseases That Spread Through Contaminated Food

Food can get contaminated if not cooked or stored properly. The contaminant of food can be a pathogen, a chemical or any other harmful substance.

Diseases that spread by the consumption of contaminated food are known as **food-borne diseases**. The common symptoms seen are nausea, vomiting, abdominal cramps and diarrhoea.

Prevention of Contamination of Food

- Before preparing or serving food, always wash your hands with soap and water.
- The dishcloths used in the kitchen should be dried properly. If left wet after use, they can harbour germs.
- The utensils used for cooking and storing food should be cleaned properly.
- Store raw meat separately and away from vegetables in a refrigerator.
- Cook meat and fish thoroughly to kill germs.

- Avoid consuming content of packed foods after the date of expiry.
- Use pasteurized milk.
- Kitchens and store rooms should be kept clean and free of cockroaches.

Diseases That Spread Through Contaminated Water

Diseases that spread due to the consumption of contaminated water or beverages are known as **water-borne diseases**. Contamination can spread through bathing, washing, drinking and preparing food with that water. Some of the common symptoms of infection are sore throat, cough, fever, diarrhoea, abdominal cramps, bloating, nausea and vomiting.

Prevention Water-borne Diseases

- Water from rivers, streams and lakes, if untreated, should not be used for consumption.
- Ice used in juices should be made from treated water or else it may be contaminated.
- Boiling water before drinking is one of the cheapest methods to get safe drinking water.
- Keep drinking water in a closed container in a clean place.

Diseases That Spread Through Direct Contact

Chickenpox, measles, ringworm, conjunctivitis, scabies and athlete's foot are some of the diseases that get transferred from an infected person to a healthy person through direct contact. Sharing clothes, bedding, utensils, etc., are some of the ways through which a healthy person can be infected.

Prevention of Diseases That Spread Through Direct Contact

- Always wash hands after using the toilet and before preparing or eating food.
- Public places like railway stations, bus stands and airports should be kept clean to prevent the spread of diseases, as people come from many different places.
- Dispose of used tissues in dustbins to avoid spreading of germs.
- Avoid sharing comb, tooth brush, soap and other personal clothing.
- Keep infected or pus-formed wounds clean and away from the contact of other people.

Diseases That Spread Through Air (Droplet Infection)

Some pathogens spread to the nearby air in the form of large respiratory droplets when an infected person sneezes, coughs or exhales. Diseases get transferred to other people who are in close vicinity of the infected person and breathe this air. Droplets that spread around stay infectious for some time. Direct contact with any substance on which these droplets are scattered shall infect the healthy individual. Common cold, diphtheria, influenza, meningitis, mumps and whooping cough are some of the common diseases that spread through droplet infection.

Prevention of Droplet Infection

- Cover the nose and mouth with a tissue paper while coughing and sneezing.
- Dispose of used tissue paper that has been used for blowing the nose, sneezing and coughing.

Diseases That Spread Through Vectors

Insects such as mosquitoes, ticks and bugs, and animals such as dogs, cats and monkeys carry pathogens. These animals are called **vectors** or **vehicles** that carry infection with them. They infect a healthy person by biting. Even though cockroaches and flies do not bite, they carry pathogens on their wings and feet.

An unhygienic environment is the perfect breeding ground for these vectors. Table 6.2 gives a list of vectors, pathogens they carry and the disease caused by these pathogen.

Do You Know?

Common cold is a minor infection of the nose and throat which can be caused by more than 200 different viruses. The most common virus that causes common cold is the *Rhinovirus*.

Table 6.2 Some vector-borne diseases

Vector	Pathogen	Disease
Female *Anopheles* mosquito	Protozoan	Malaria
Aedes mosquito	Virus	Dengue, Chikungunya
House flies	Bacterium	Cholera
	Bacterium	Typhoid
	Protozoan	Dysentery
Louse or ticks	Bacterium	Typhus fever

▲ Fig. 6.5 Female *Anopheles* mosquito

▲ Fig. 6.6 House fly

▲ Fig. 6.7 Louse

Prevention of Spread of Diseases Through Vectors

- By cleaning unhygienic surroundings and clearing stagnant water and heaps of garbage, we can reduce many infections and diseases.
- If your surroundings are not hygienic, they can house cockroaches, mosquitoes, rats, stray dogs, etc. These insects and animals are responsible for causing many diseases.
- To protect oneself from mosquito bites, one must wear full-sleeve clothes. Use mosquito repellents at homes and mosquito nets while sleeping.
- Get the anti-rabies vaccination immediately if bitten by a dog.
- Use insecticides at home to avoid cockroaches, houseflies and ants.
- Cover prepared food and drinking water to avoid the spread of infection due to houseflies.
- Avoid eating from road-side vendors or eateries.

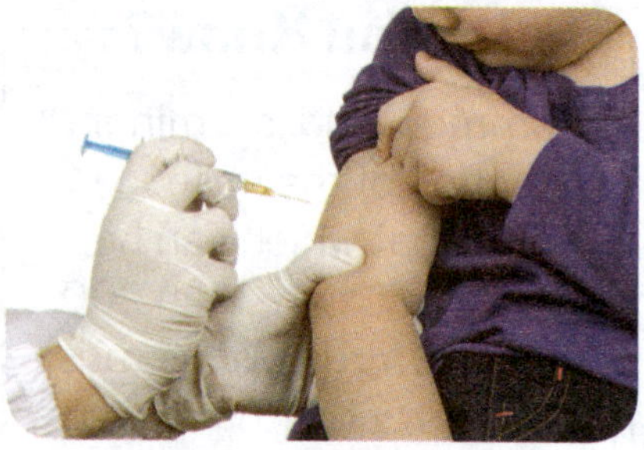

▲ Fig. 6.8 Vaccination

Prevention of Diseases through Vaccination

Vaccines are substances that can be administered to the body to prevent diseases like polio, measles, mumps, diphtheria, hepatitis and tetanus. This process is called **vaccination**. Vaccination protects a person by not allowing the germs to multiply in case they enter the body. Many communicable diseases can be prevented from spreading by vaccinations at the right time. Most of the vaccines are administered to a baby during the initial months after the birth of a baby to protect it against diseases.

Know the Scientist

Edward Jenner (1749–1823) was an English physician who pioneered the invention of the smallpox vaccine, which was a dreadful disease during the late 1700s and early 1800s. He is famously called 'the father of immunology' for his work.

Revision Zone

Match the following.

1. Malaria	a. Droplet infection
2. Chickenpox	b. Contaminated food and water
3. Cholera	c. Vector
4. Influenza	d. Direct contact

Personal Hygiene

Personal hygiene are practices followed to keep oneself clean. In addition to good diet, adequate sleep and exercise, cleanliness is also essential to keep oneself healthy.

Some of the personal hygiene practices are as follows.

- Bathe regularly to remove dust, sweat and dirt from the body, and cleanse the body from harmful microbes.
- Wash hands frequently, especially before and after using the toilet, before and after having meals, and after touching animals, dustbins and wounds to prevent germs from spreading.
- Brush your teeth twice a day.
- Clip your nails regularly.
- Wash and comb hair regularly to keep the scalp clean, and free of dust and germs. It also prevents dandruff and head lice.
- Wear clean clothes, especially clean undergarments and socks. This is a good practice to keep the body clean.
- Cover mouth while coughing to prevent germs from spreading.

▲ Fig. 6.9 Washing hands

▲ Fig. 6.10 Brushing teeth

▲ Fig. 6.11 Clipping nails

Care of Eyes

Our eyes have eyelashes, the mechanism of continuous blinking to protect them from dust and dirt, and tears to wash away the dirt particles. These are the natural mechanisms for protecting our eyes. Following are some of the things we can do to take care of our eyes.

- Wash the eyes with cold water first thing in the morning.
- Do not read with dim light and do not keep the book very close while reading.
- Do not watch television, mobile phone, computer and laptop for a very long period.
- In case any substance, like dust particles, enters the eyes, do not rub them. Instead, wash them with plenty of cold water.
- Use sunglasses or protection glass for the eyes while going out in direct sunlight.
- Eat lots of fruits and vegetables like spinach, cabbage, papaya, carrot and mango that are rich in vitamin A. This helps in keeping the eyes healthy.
- Treat any infection in the eyes and its surrounding areas immediately.

Tech Info

For an infected eye, an ophthalmologist generally prescribes an eye drop that is to be applied at regular intervals of time. Only 7 per cent of the medicine gets absorbed into the eye through the drops while the rest drips out. Scientists from the Harvard medical college have invented 'medicated contact lenses' made out of biodegradable polymer mixed with antibiotics. The utilization of medicine through lenses is 100 per cent as compared to eye drops.

Care of Teeth

Maintaining oral hygiene helps in protection of the teeth and gums, and prevents tooth decay. Following are some of the methods that can be adopted to take care of our teeth.

- Brush teeth regularly twice a day, that is, after waking up in the morning and before going to bed at night.
- Follow the correct pattern of brushing, that is, the brush should move from gum to enamel and it should reach all the surfaces of the teeth.
- Use a good quality toothbrush with soft bristles. Change the toothbrush in every three to four months.
- Massaging gums and teeth after brushing increases the circulation of blood to the roots of the teeth.
- Wash the mouth thoroughly before and after having food. Use a good mouthwash.
- A balanced diet is essential for healthy teeth and gums. Avoid eating too many chocolates and toffees.

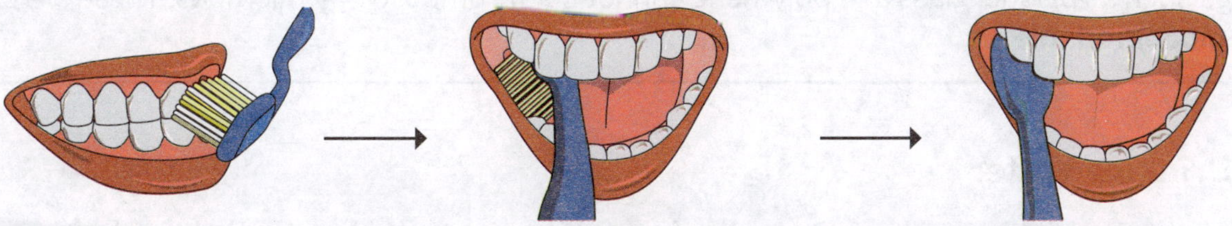

▲ Fig. 6.12 Teeth should be brushed properly to keep them healthy

Care of Hair

It is important to maintain healthy hair as it adds beauty to the external appearance of an individual. Following are some ways to take care of hair.

- Wash and shampoo the hair regularly, twice or thrice a week.
- Keep the scalp clean and dry. Comb your hair daily with a soft hairbrush or comb. Massage the scalp with a good hair oil regularly to improve hair growth.
- Drink plenty of water and eat a balanced diet for healthy hair.

Community Hygiene

Clean surroundings help us to stay healthy. Civic bodies like panchayats in villages and municipal corporations in cities are responsible for keeping the surroundings clean. But we, as responsible citizens, should also play our part in keeping our surroundings clean. Following are some steps we can take to ensure this.

- Cleanliness of the city begins with the cleanliness of individual homes. Always keep your home clean.
- Do not litter your surroundings. Keep separate bins for biodegradable and non-biodegradable wastes. Always throw the garbage in the specific bins.
- Always keep garbage bins closed. Hand over these bins to garbage collectors or empty them in specific places fixed for dumping garbage.
- Maintain clean water outlets. Do not let dirty water from the kitchen or toilet flow out into open areas.
- Do not throw plastic and glass in drains. Fix any blocked drains immediately.
- Check sewage pipes regularly for any leakage or damage.

Green bin

Blue bin

▲ Fig. 6.13 Segregation of wastes in different bins

Biodegradable vs Non-biodegradable

Things that can be decomposed by microbes are called **biodegradable**. All animal and plant matter (vegetable and fruit peels, leaves and twigs, dead plants and animals, etc.) are biodegradable. Things such as plastic, glass and polythene cannot be decomposed by microbes. These are called **non-biodegradable**.

Safe Drinking Water

Clean and safe drinking water is essential for maintaining good health. Dirty water contaminated with germs can cause many diseases. Water-borne diseases can cause epidemics because the whole population of a city or town might be drinking water from the same source. Following are some of the methods that can be used to get clean water.

- **Boiling**: Boil the water for 10–15 minutes and cool to room temperature before consuming it. This kills the harmful germs in water.
- **Chlorination**: It involves adding chlorine tablets in water to kill harmful microorganisms present in it.
- **Water filters**: Nowadays, good-quality purifiers, UV light filters and reverse osmosis (RO) filters are available that can remove physical, chemical and microbial impurities from water.

(a) Boiling

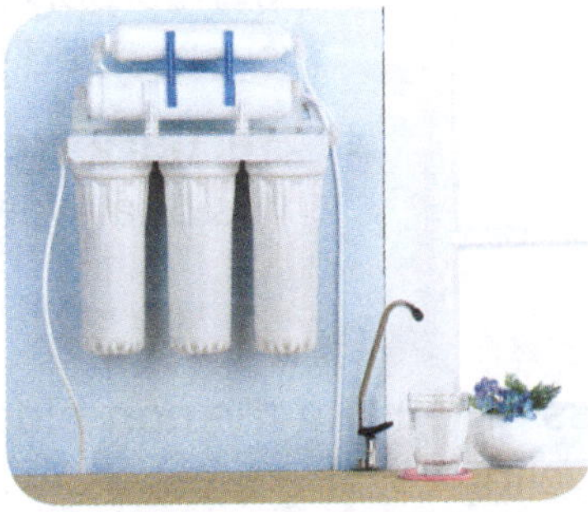

(b) UV light water filter

▲ Fig. 6.14 Water purification

Do You Know?

Water that is free from germs and fit for human consumption is called **potable water**.

Waste Disposal

Effective disposal of waste is necessary to maintain a clean community. Civic bodies should ensure that waste generated from households and industries is disposed of properly. Following are some of the commonly-practised waste disposal methods.

Dumping: Solid garbage is dumped in the low-lying lands, which are far away from the urban areas. These lands are covered with soil and sand, and left undisturbed for many years. Later, these lands develop into public utility areas like malls, parks, etc.

▲ Fig. 6.15 Dumping of solid garbage

Composting: This is a cost-effective and environment-friendly method of waste disposal. Compost is prepared by digging pits that are filled with waste food, garden trash, paper, pet waste, coffee grounds, agricultural waste, animal waste, etc. These pits are then covered with soil and left for some time. The waste is decomposed by the microorganisms. Earthworms added to these pits can speed up the decomposition process. This method is called **vermicomposting**.

Kitchen waste + garden waste + animal dung

Compost

▲ Fig. 6.16 Composting

Compost as Manure

The compost prepared can be used as manure in farms. This can reduce the need for chemical fertilizers.

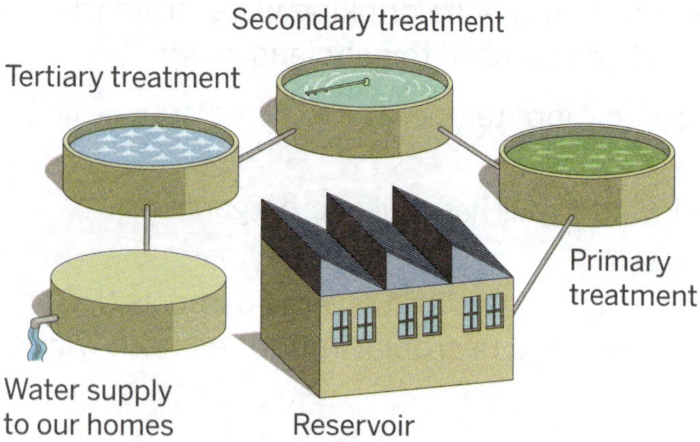

▲ Fig. 6.17 Sewage treatment plant

Sewage treatment: Solid waste and other impurities in the sewage are removed and treated by different methods to obtain purified potable water in sewage treatment plants. Treatment is done in three different stages.

1. **Primary treatment** involves removal of heavy solid wastes.
2. **Secondary treatment** involves addition of microorganisms and dissolving the suspended particles.
3. **Tertiary treatment** involves removal of residual waste and disinfecting the water.

Waste Recycling

Recycling can be defined as the process of reusing the non-biodegradable materials by changing them into new products. Recycling old products uses less energy and resources than the preparation of new products of the same kind. For instance, waste plastic water bottles can be recycled to form new toys for children.

Greenathon

Segregate your garbage into compostable, recyclable and that which needs to be sent to the garbage dump. Put all the biodegradable wastes in the compost pit. The recyclable group can be given to a *kabadiwallah*. You can also find ways to reuse a few of the materials from the non-biodegradable waste.

▲ Fig. 6.18 Recycling non-biodegradable products

Revision Zone

Match the following.

1. Vitamin A
2. Chlorination
3. Filters
4. Composting
5. Recycling

a. Reverse osmosis of water
b. Organic manure
c. Solid waste management
d. Kills microorganisms
e. Enhances eyesight

Keywords

Non-communicable diseases: diseases that cannot spread from one person to another

Communicable diseases: diseases that can spread from one person to another

Pathogens: microorganisms that cause diseases, also known as germs

Vectors: animals or insects that carry pathogens in their bodies

Hygiene: a practice of cleanliness that is essential to maintain good health

Biodegradable: substances that can be broken down into smaller units by the action of microbes

Non-biodegradable: substances that cannot be broken down into smaller pieces by the action of microbes

Compost: end product of the composting process, which can be used as manure

In a Nutshell

- Diseases that spread from an infected person to a healthy person are known as communicable diseases.
- Communicable diseases spread through direct contact, contaminated food and water, vectors and air droplets.
- Bacteria, fungi, virus and protozoa are the four groups of microbes that cause diseases in humans.
- Various precautionary steps need to be adopted in order to prevent infection from pathogens through various modes.
- Maintaining personal hygiene prevents an individual from infections. This can be achieved by frequent washing of hands, brushing teeth twice a day, bathing, etc.
- Biodegradable and non-biodegradable wastes need to be separated and disposed of accordingly.
- Biodegradable wastes can be converted to manure and fertilizers by composting them. Sewage water can be treated in the sewage treatment plants for getting clean, potable water. Inorganic wastes need to be recycled for reusing the same.
- The immediate help given to a person who has suffered an injury before the doctor arrives is called first aid. Basic knowledge of first help is necessary to help people who get injured.

Mind Map

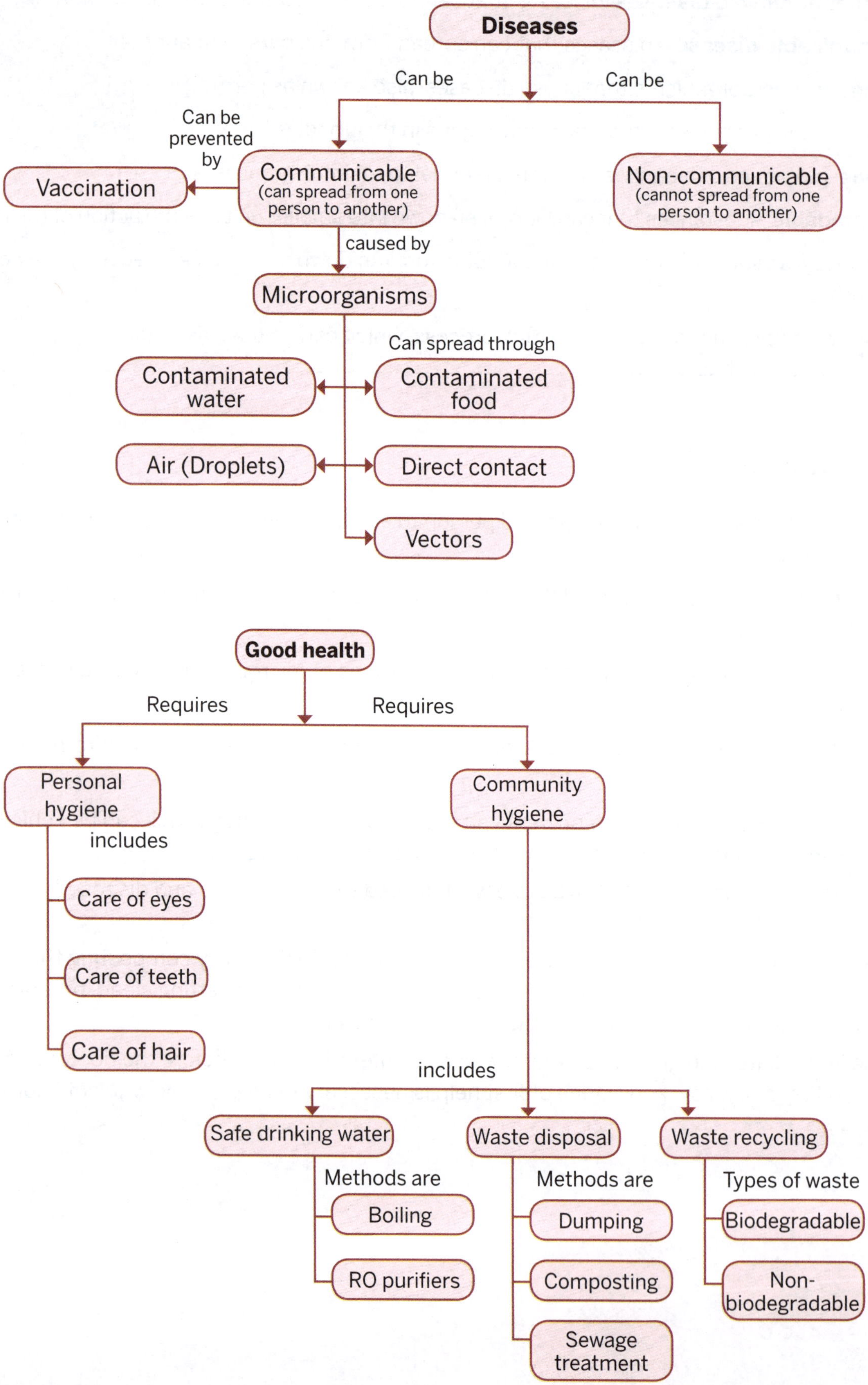

Diseases
Can be
Can be
Communicable
(can spread from one person to another)
Non-communicable
(cannot spread from one person to another)
Can be prevented by
Vaccination
caused by
Microorganisms
Can spread through
Contaminated water
Contaminated food
Air (Droplets)
Direct contact
Vectors
Good health
Requires
Requires
Personal hygiene
includes
Care of eyes
Care of teeth
Care of hair
Community hygiene
includes
Safe drinking water
Methods are
Boiling
RO purifiers
Waste disposal
Methods are
Dumping
Composting
Sewage treatment
Waste recycling
Types of waste
Biodegradable
Non-biodegradable

Exercise

1 Choose the correct answer for each of the following.

a. Diseases that can spread from one person to another are called ________ diseases.

i. Communicable ii. Genetic
iii. Non-communicable iv. None of these

b. Which of the following diseases is not transmitted through contact?

i. Ringworm ii. Scabies
iii. Measles iv. Malaria

c. Which of the following diseases spread through droplet infection

i. Malaria ii. Polio
iii. Common cold iv. Cholera

d. Which of the following disease spreads through contaminated food

i. Cholera ii. Measles
iii. Polio iv. Dengue

e. Which of the following is a water-borne disease?

i. Chickenpox ii. Typhoid
iii. Influenza iv. Rabies

f. Identify the right way of garbage disposal.

i. Dumping into water bodies
ii. Dumping on the road side
iii. Dumping in pits and covering
iv. Dumping around the home

g. Which among the following vitamins helps in improving eyesight?

i. Vitamin B ii. Vitamin C
iii. Vitamin D iv. Vitamin A

h. Identify the habit that is not a hygienic practice.

i. Washing hands regularly
ii. Keeping good oral health
iii. Using clothes without washing
iv. Bathing regularly

i. The practices followed to keep oneself clean are called

i. community hygiene practices
ii. meditation practices
iii. personal hygiene practices
iv. oral hygiene practices

j. Which of these is not a method of water purification?

i. Boiling ii. Chlorination
iii. Nitrification iv. Using RO filters

2 Fill in the blanks.

a. Dengue and chikungunya are caused by __________ (*Aedes/ Anopheles*) mosquito.

b. Substances administered to the body to prevent diseases is called __________ (protection/vaccination).

c. Disease causing microorganisms are called __________ (vectors/ pathogens).

d. Animals that carry pathogens are called __________ (vectors/virus).

e. Chickenpox spreads through __________ (contaminated water/ direct contact).

f. Massaging gums and teeth after brushing __________ (decrease/ increases) the circulation of blood.

g. __________ (Panchayat/Municipal corporation) is responsible for keeping villages clean.

3 Write T for True and F for False.

a. Bacteria, virus, fungi and protozoa are the four types of pathogens.

b. Sharing personal things increases the risk of infection through direct contact.

c. Malaria spreads through the bite of *Aedes* mosquito.
d. Tuberculosis is caused by a virus.
e. Rabies spreads by the bite of dogs.
f. Unhygienic surrounds can house vectors like mosquitoes, flies, cockroaches, etc.
g. Good hygiene and proper sanitation prevents harmful microorganisms from causing diseases.
h. Eating fruits and vegetables like papaya and carrot keeps the eyes healthy.
i. Cleanliness of the city begins with the cleanliness of individual homes.

4 Define the following.

a. Communicable diseases
b. Non-communicable diseases
c. Vaccination
d. Personal hygiene

5 Differentiate between the following.

a. Communicable and non-communicable diseases
b. Pathogens and vectors
c. Droplet infection and water borne infection
d. Food-borne and water-borne diseases

6 Answer the following questions in brief.

a. Write a note on droplet infection.
b. What are vectors?
c. What are the ways to prevent food-borne diseases?
d. Write a short note on vaccination.
e. Explain any two methods of waste disposal.
f. Write any two ways to purify water.

7 Answer the following questions in detail.

a. Write a note on diseases that spread through direct contact.
b. What are food-borne diseases? How can they be prevented?
c. What are vector-borne diseases? How can they be prevented?
d. Write a note on the importance of clean surroundings.
e. Write a note on personal hygiene.
f. Give any five ways in which one can take care of eyes.
g. Give any five ways in which one can take care of teeth.
h. Give any three ways in which one can take care of hair.

8 Think and answer.

a. Microorganisms are found everywhere, even inside our body. Then why do we not fall sick all the time?
b. Raju's little brother is in Class 3. He is suffering from measles, but still wants to go to school. Their mother said he should stay at home till he recovers completely. Why did she say so?

9 Thinking Beyond

a. Acquired Immunodeficiency Syndrome (AIDS) is a fatal diseases. Find out why no cure for it has been found so far.
b. Nowadays, UV and RO water filters have become popular. Ultraviolet (UV) light has the capacity to kill harmful microorganisms. Reverse osmosis (RO) is a technique used for making water potable using a semipermeable membrane.

   Find out more about these filters and compare the two types of filters based on the mechanism used, contaminants removed and cost effectiveness.

10 Project

a. Conduct a survey in your neighbourhood. Interview 20 children and find out how frequently they eat food from restaurants or roadside vendors. Record your findings in the format of the table given below:

Name	Age	Frequency of eating food from outside				Have you ever fallen ill after consuming food from outside?
		Never	Rarely	Once or twice a week	Almost everyday	

What conclusions can you draw from the survey?

b. Place colour-specific garbage bins in the school. Blue garbage bins for the collection of non-biodegradable waste, green garbage bins for the collection of biodegradable waste and yellow garbage bins for the collection of infectious waste like used cotton and other medical wastes.

Worksheet

1 Subject Integration

List some of the food items and simple exercises for different organs of the human body which are good for the overall health and development of the body. One is done for you.

Organ	Food	Exercise
Eye	Carrots	Rolling of eyes, ample rest

2 Life Skills

A clean environment is essential in order to stay healthy. List five ways in the space given below by which you will keep your surroundings clean.

____

____

____

____

____

____

Adaptation

7

What I shall learn

- Habitat
- Adaptations
- Adaptations of plants and animals in aquatic habitat, deserts, mountains and in air

▲ Fig. 7.1: Grassland

▲ Fig. 7.2: Mountain

▲ Fig. 7.3: Forest

Habitats

The place where an organism lives naturally is called its ***habitat***. It provides the organism with suitable conditions to live and reproduce. Plants and animals often share the same habitat.

A large variety of plants and animals live in various habitats. Let us learn more about these habitats, and the plants and animals that live there.

Terrestrial Habitats

Habitats on land are called ***terrestrial habitats***. Accordingly, the animals that live on land are called terrestrial animals. Some terrestrial habitats are discussed below.

Grasslands

This region is dominated by grass, small trees and shrubs. Grasslands get moderate rain, and are usually windy and dry. Some of the animals that can be found in a grassland are zebra, giraffe, deer, tiger and lion.

Mountains

Mountains are habitats found at higher altitudes. They are usually extremely cold and windy.

Depending on the altitude, these regions sometimes experience snowfall as the temperature decreases. Some animals that can be found in a mountain habitat are yak, sheep, mountain goat, etc.

Forests

Forests habitats are usually dominated by the presence of a large number of plants and trees.

Animals living in forests exhibit a wide variety of relationships to survive. One such example is the predator–prey relationship seen between the lion and the deer.

▲ Fig. 7.4: Desert

Deserts

Deserts are sandy lands with scanty rainfall. Most deserts get less than 10 inches of rainfall each year, and are very hot and dry. Deserts that are hot during the day may become cold at night. Some deserts are always cold like the Gobi desert in Asia and the desert in the continent of Antarctica. The largest hot desert in the world is the Sahara in Africa, which experiences temperatures of up to 122 degrees Fahrenheit (50 degrees Celsius) during the day.

Plant life in the deserts include cacti and some thorny plants. Animals usually found in the deserts are camels, kangaroo rats, rattle snakes, etc.

▲ Fig. 7.5: Polar region

Polar Regions

Polar regions are covered with snow and are very cold for most parts of the year. During winter, the temperatures can go as low as −37°C.

Animals that can be found in the polar regions are polar bears, penguins, seals and walruses.

Aquatic Habitats

Habitats in water are described as ***aquatic habitats***. Some examples of aquatic habitats are discussed below.

▲ Fig. 7.6: Freshwater habitat

Freshwater Habitat

Freshwater habitats include rivers, streams, canals, lakes and ponds. Various types of fish, frogs, lotus and water lilies can be found in freshwater habitats.

Marine Habitat

These are saltwater habitats, for example, coasts and oceans. Marine habitats are home to a large variety of plants and animals. Planktons, seaweeds, fish, whales, crabs, octopuses, turtles and starfish live here.

Estuaries: These are coastal regions where a river or stream containing freshwater meets the salty water of the sea. Horseshoe crabs, mangroves and sea grass are found in estuaries. Hundreds of fish and shellfish such as shrimp and salmon live in estuaries.

Coral reefs: A coral reef is a community of underwater creatures called corals, which provide a habitat for plants, fish and many other animals. They are made up of hard and soft corals. Sponges, lobsters, snails, octopuses, fish, sea turtles, sharks, dolphin, etc. form a part of this community.

Revision Zone

State whether the following statements are True (T) or False (F).

1. A habitat consists of both biotic (living) and abiotic (non-living) components.
2. Mountains are habitats found at lower altitudes.
3. Oceans and coasts are examples of freshwater habitats.
4. Polar regions are covered with snow for most parts of the year.
5. Estuaries and coral reefs are examples of desert habitats.

Adaptations

The desert and the sea are two extremely different habitats having different kinds of plants and organisms. When we compare the organisms found in the desert and the sea, e.g., camel and shark, respectively, we find that their body structures and features are different because they are meant to live in different habitats.

*The features and habits of plants and animals that enable them to survive in their surroundings are called **adaptations**.*

Let us now study the adaptations of different plants and animals to survive in their respective habitats.

Adaptations for Deserts

Some adaptations shown by plants and animals living in deserts are given below:

Plants: Different kinds of cacti inhabit deserts. Plants adapted to live in desert conditions are called **xerophytes**.

▲ Fig. 7.7 Plants and animals in a desert

Some common adaptations seen among plants of this region are as follows:

1. **Roots**: The sandy soil cannot hold water, so the water is stored at a very low level below the ground. The plants growing in these regions have very long roots, which can penetrate deep into the soil in search of water.
2. **Stems**: Many cacti have fleshy stems that store water and a thick waxy layer that helps to retain water.

3. **Leaves**: To reduce the loss of water due to transpiration, the leaves of cacti are modified into spines, which also prevents predators from feeding on them. The process of photosynthesis is taken up by the fleshy stems.

Animals: Deserts are home to reptiles, insects and small mammals. Animals such as camels, rats, snakes live in these habitat. Some common adaptations are as follows:

1. They have thick skins with fewer pores.
2. They hardly sweat and excrete less urine in order to retain water in their body.
3. Some adaptations specific to few animals are given below:
   (a) **Camels**: Camels have long legs and thick skin to stay away from the heat of the sand. They can drink a large amount of water at a time and can stay without water for long periods of time. They have a hump on their back to store fat.
   (b) **Rats and snakes**: They burrow under the sand during daytime to stay away from the heat. They restrict their movement during the day and hunt for prey during the night.
4. Desert animals are adapted to be active during early mornings and late evenings when the temperature is moderate, and they rest during the day when it is the hottest.
5. These animals have less fur and very little body fat, which allows them to lose heat through their skin surface.
6. Other desert animals are adapted to drink very little water or get it from the food they eat.

Adaptations for Mountains

▲ Fig. 7.8 Plants and animals in mountains

Some adaptations shown by plants and animals living in mountains are given below:

Plants: The foothills of mountains contain plenty of trees. As we go up the mountains, plants are adapted to the harsh climate. Several trees like the pine and fir grow in this region.

Towards the top of the mountain, coniferous trees are prevalent as they are much better at dealing with the cold weather. At very high altitudes, like those on the mountaintops, the surface is covered with snow and ice, and very few plants can survive.

Some common adaptations of such plants are as follows:

1. Trees grow tall to trap sunlight.
2. Leaves are small and needle shaped.
3. Conical shape of the trees with sloping branches allows the snow to slide down easily.

Animals: Animals such as yaks, mountain sheep, mountain goats, snow leopards and llamas are adapted to the mountainous habitats as they are **sure-footed**, that is, they can walk with ease on unsteady paths of the mountains. They have thick woolly furs to survive the cold weather.

Some common adaptations of animals living in mountains are listed below:

1. They have thick fur covering their body to protect them from cold weather.

2. Some animals like the yak and mountain goat have long hair all over their body to protect them from the cold weather.
3. Strong hooves of mountain sheep, goats and yaks help them to walk on the slopes of the mountains.
4. During the winter season, the animals living in these habitats move less and conserve their energy by hibernating or migrating down from the mountains.

Adaptations For Aquatic Habitat

Plants and animals that live in water develop special adaptive features to help them grow and survive. The more time they spend in water, the more adapted the organisms are to survive in the aquatic habitat.

Freshwater plants are called **hydrophytes**.

▲ Fig. 7.9 Animals in an ocean habitat

Aquatic Plants

Plants that grow and live in water are called **aquatic plants**. The following figure shows the different types of aquatic plants.

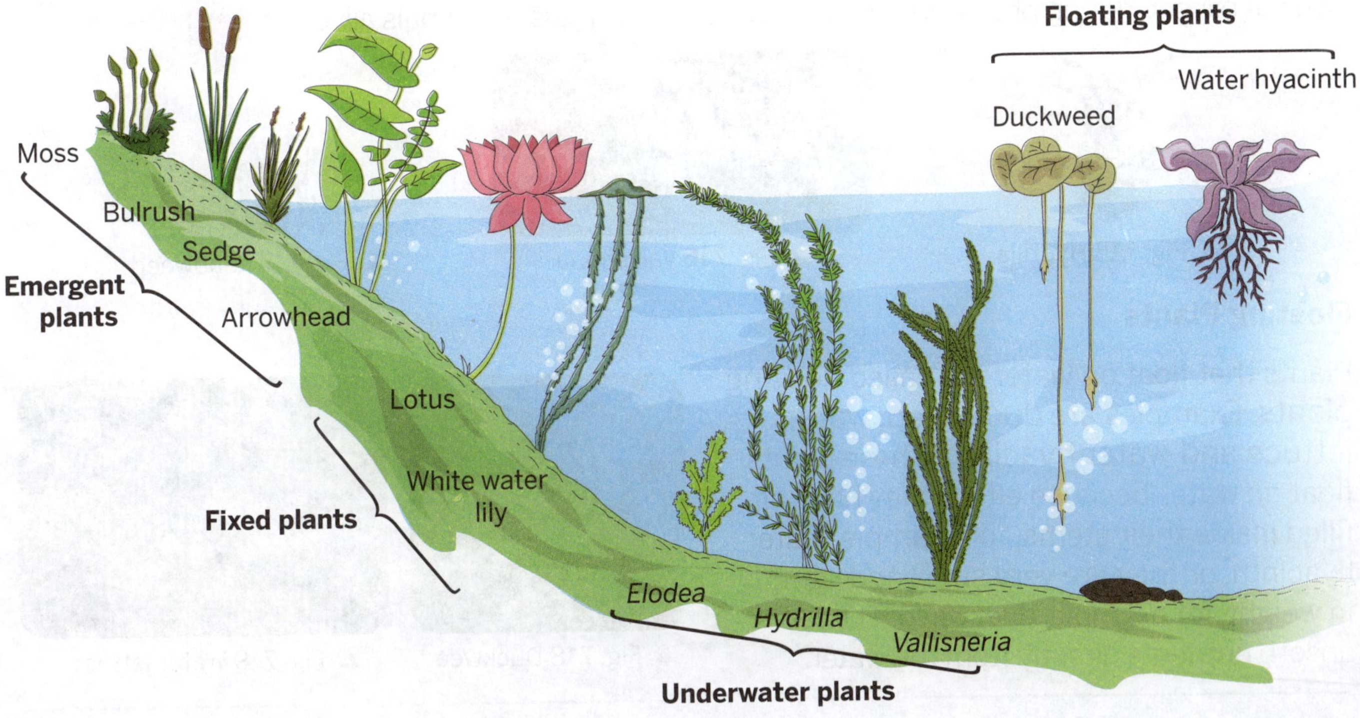

▲ Fig. 7.10 Aquatic plants

Emergent Plants

Some water plants are called emergent plants because even when their roots are fixed in the soil of the shallow waterbed, their leaves and stems extend out of the surface of the water body they are growing in. Examples of emergent plants are bulrush (cattail) arrowhead and sedge.

▲ Fig. 7.11 Bulrush

▲ Fig. 7.12 Sedge

▲ Fig. 7.13 Lotus

▲ Fig. 7.14 Water lily

Fixed Plants

These plants are fixed to the waterbed with the help of strong roots. Hence, they are called fixed plants. Examples are lotus and water lily. They have thin, long stalks that are hollow and light in weight. These keep the flowers and leaves floating on the surface of the water. The leaves of these plants have a waxy coating that prevents them from getting wet. The leaves have stomata on the upper side instead of the lower side. Fixed plants absorb nutrients from the soil in the waterbeds through their roots.

Underwater Plants

These plants grow and remain completely submerged into the water. Hence, they are also called submerged plants. Examples are *Hydrilla*, *Vallisneria* and pondweed. They have thin, narrow, ribbon-like leaves to prevent them from getting torn by the force of water currents.

The leaves of underwater plants do not have stomata but they take in carbon dioxide from the water through their body surface. These plants do not bear flowers. They get nutrients through the roots from the soil in the waterbeds. Underwater plants support animal life to a great extent because they give out oxygen during photosynthesis, which keeps the aquatic animals alive.

▲ Fig. 7.15 Hydrilla

▲ Fig. 7.16 Vallisneria

▲ Fig. 7.17 Pondweed

Floating Plants

Plants that float on water are called floating plants. Examples are duckweed, water lettuce and water hyacinth. These plants float on water because either they have air filled inside their stems, for example, water hyacinth, or they are very small and light in weight, for example, duckweed. The roots absorb nutrients directly from the water.

▲ Fig. 7.18 Duckweed

▲ Fig. 7.19 Water lettuce

Revision Zone

State whether the following statements are true (T) or false (F).

1. Water lettuce floats on water.
2. Sedges are fixed in water and hence are called fixed plants.
3. Fixed plants have stomata on the upper side of their leaves.
4. Duckweed is an example of emergent plant.
5. The arrowhead plants have leaves and stems emerging out of the water surface.

Aquatic Animals

Fish, some snakes and frogs are found in freshwater habitats. Frogs use their long legs and webbed feet to swim. Crabs, prawns, sharks and whales are found in saltwater habitats. Octopuses live in the deep waters of the oceans.

Big and small fish of different types are found in both saltwater and freshwater habitats. Let us learn about the main adaptations in fish that help them to live in aquatic habitat.

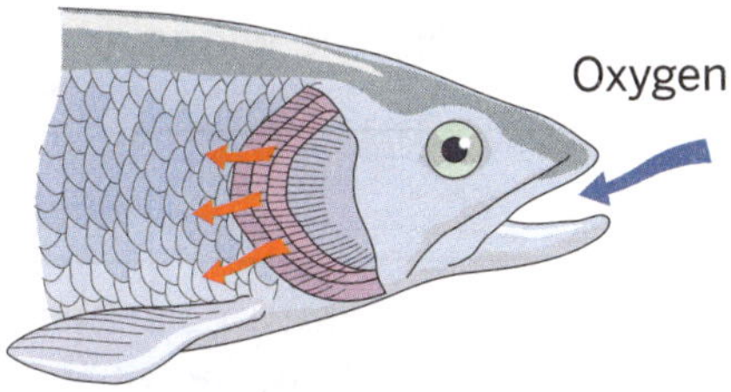

▲ Fig. 7.20 Gills in fish

Respiration in Fish

Aquatic animals like fish live in water and obtain oxygen, which is dissolved in water. Fish have a special structure called **gills** for respiration on either side of their mouth. The water along with dissolved oxygen enters the mouth and the absorption of oxygen takes place through the gills. Carbon dioxide diffuses in the water, which is released through the openings in the gills.

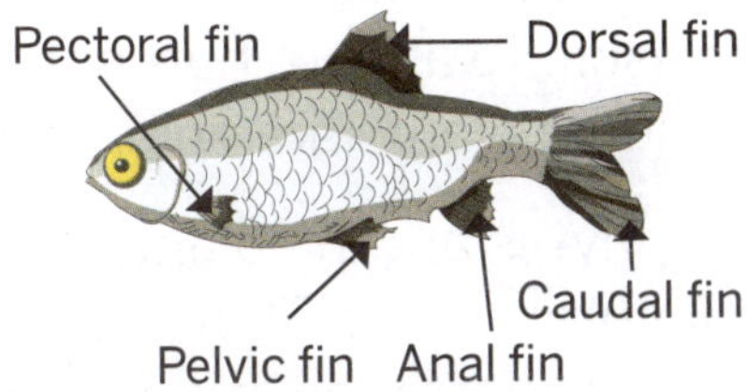

▲ Fig. 7.21 Paired and unpaired fins in fish

Movement in Fish

Fish are vertebrates that live in water. The body of a fish has a streamlined shape, that is, it is broad in the middle and narrow at the two ends, like a boat. This helps the fish to cut through the water easily. It has an internal skeleton, which is attached to strong muscles.

The fins too have skeletal and muscular support. It swims by curving its body and tail muscles. These curves cause its body to twist and turn, pushing the fish forward. It changes its direction, balances and swims with the help of its fins.

Fish have two types of fins: **paired** (pelvic and pectoral fins) and **unpaired** (dorsal, caudal and anal fins). The unpaired fins help in forward and backward movement and in taking turns. The paired fins help in upward and downward movement, maintain the position of the fish at rest and act like brakes in a vehicle. A special structure called a **swim bladder** is present in most fish. It can be filled with air or emptied out to move up and down in water.

Adaptations for Aerial Habitat

Movement in Bird

Birds fly in the air and walk on the ground. Some birds can only walk. Birds such as ducks and swans can swim, while there are some birds such as ostrich and kiwi that cannot fly but are good runners.

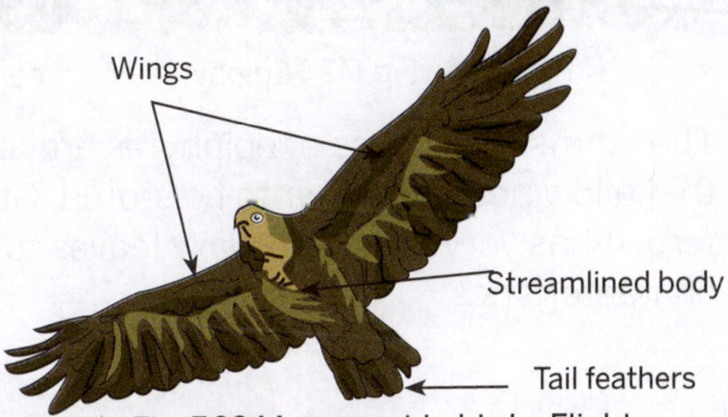

▲ Fig. 7.22 Movement in birds: Flight

The birds that can fly have hollow, lightweight bones. Wings, feathers and specialized muscles attached to the wings help them in flying. The body shape of flying birds is streamlined, which helps them to move against the direction of wind. Birds show two types of flight—flapping and gliding movements.

In **flapping flight**, the wings are actively flapped up and down to propel the bird forward or maintain balance. You can see this in birds such as sparrows and mynahs.

Gliding and **soaring** are seen in large birds such as eagles and kites. If you observe an eagle or a kite in flight, you will see that its wings are kept spread as it appears to move effortlessly in air. During gliding, the wings are flapped occasionally.

Discuss

What are the features in birds that help them in flight? Which of these features are not likely to be seen in flightless birds?

Aerial Plants

Aerial plants have roots above the ground, i.e., the roots of these plants are not attached to the soil. To absorb nutrients, these plants have developed hanging roots. A common example of aerial plants are epiphytes.

Epiphytes are the plants that grow mainly on the twigs, trunks, and even the leaves of rainforest trees. They are not rooted in the soil nor are they parasitic (i.e., they do not directly harm the other plant). The roots of these plants are not in soil. Examples are orchids, philodendrons, ferns and bromeliads.

Adaptations in Epiphytes

▲ Fig. 7.23 Epiphytes on a tree

1. Epiphytes have adapted to live on the branches of tall trees so that they are able to access sunlight that plants on lower levels of a rainforest canopy cannot.
2. Epiphytes have a strong, thick root system that is extremely efficient in absorbing water from mist, rain and atmospheric humidity.
3. Unlike most plants that live in soil, epiphytes' roots obtain nutrients from leaf litter and other debris that accumulate on the branches of trees they live on.

The stems and leaves of epiphytes are also modified. Bromeliads have stiff, upturned leaves that allow pools of water to be stored. Other types of modified leaves include our Staghorn fern. It has very thick and waxy leaves to retain moisture. Many epiphytes' stems share similar characteristics.

Acclimatization

When people climb mountains, they find it hard to breathe and the body feels heavy to carry out any activity. This is because the body is not adjusted to the changes in that particular environment. At higher altitudes, the volume of oxygen present in air is less than what one gets on flat lands. So, the body has to work harder to produce energy. As days go by, the body begins to adjust to the changes on the mountain making breathing much easier and the body becomes more active.

*The adjustment made by the body to overcome chronic changes in the surrounding environment within a short time is called **acclimatization**.*

Changes include oxygen availability, temperature, moisture and food. Every change in the environment requires acclimatization by living organisms. Acclimatization and adaptation are not the same, but they are similar. The differences are that acclimatization is temporary, but adaptation is a permanent change; acclimatization refers to the adjustments to be made while adaptation is the adjustment already made. For example, humans may be adapted to live in mountains, but many have to become acclimatized to the prevalent conditions.

Keywords

Habitat: The place where an organism naturally lives

Adaptation: Special features or habits in an organism that helps it to survive in its surroundings

Fixed Plants: Plants that are fixed to the waterbed with the help of strong roots

Underwater Plants: Plants that grow and remain completely submerged into the water

Xerophytes: Plants those are adapted to live in desert conditions

Aerial Plants: Plants that have roots above the ground

Acclimatization: The adjustment made by the body to overcome chronic changes in the surrounding environment within a short time

In a Nutshell

- Habitat provides the organism with the suitable conditions to live and reproduce.
- The features and habits of plants and animals that enable them to live and survive in their surroundings are called adaptation.
- Aquatic plants adapt themselves by developing special features to either float or stay completely under the water.
- Aquatic animals like fish live in water and obtain oxygen which is dissolved in water.
- Plants adapted to live in deserts have special structures like long roots, fleshy stems and the spines that are modified from leaves.
- Birds capable of flying exhibit gliding or flapping flight
- Aerial plants have roots above the ground. The roots of these plants are not attached to soil. To absorb nutrients these plants have developed '*hanging roots*'.

Exercise

1 Choose the correct answer for each of the following.

a. A camel has long legs to __________.
   i. walk fast on the sand
   ii. walk slowly on the sand
   iii. keep its body away from the heat
   iv. run on the sand

b. The thick and waxy stem in a cactus plant helps in __________.
   i. storing water
   ii. absorbing water
   iii. retaining water
   iv. reducing loss of water

c. Animals living in mountainous regions have __________.
   i. strong beaks ii. long legs
   iii. thick fur iv. a hump

d. The trees that grow in mountainous regions have __________.
   i. cone-shaped and short branches
   ii. curved-shaped and sloping branches
   iii. curved-shaped and long branches
   iv. cone-shaped and sloping branches

e. The needle-like leaves of mountain trees help in __________.
   i. absorption of water
   ii. sliding off the snow
   iii. making the trees look attractive
   iv. absorbing sunlight

f. Plant that floats in water is __________.
   i. Duckweed ii. Pondweed
   iii. Water lily iv. Hydrilla

g. Which of the following is a xerophyte?
   i. Cactus ii. Teak
   iii. Palm iv. All of them

2 Fill in the blanks.

a. The function of spines in desert plants is to __________.(reduce water loss/ attract insects)

b. Animals living in mountainous regions are adapted to live in __________ climate.(warm/cold)

c. The habitat of frogs is __________. (pond/trees)

d. Desert snakes and rats come out mostly during the __________. (day/ night)

e. Fish absorb oxygen from water using their __________. (nostrils/gills)

f. The plant that shows adaptation to air is called as __________. (epiphytes/ xerophytes)

g. Arrowhead is an example of plant __________. (floating/emergent)

3 Write T for True and F for False.

a. The spines in the cactus plants are the modified leaves.

b. Desert climates are hot during the day and cold during the night.

c. Animals such as zebra and giraffe are found in deserts.

d. Desert plants are called xerophytes.

e. Water lily is a floating plant.

4 Define the following.

a. Habitat

b. Adaptation

c. Xerophytes

d. Gills

e. Fixed plants

5 Differentiate between the following.

a. Adaptation and acclimatization

b. Floating plants and aerial plants

c. Paired fins and unpaired fins of fish

d. Aquatic animals and animals that live in deserts

e. Flapping movement and gliding movement of birds

6 Choose the odd one out. Give reasons for the choice.

a. Duckweed; water lettuce; lotus; water hyacinth

b. Vallisneria; pondweed; Hydrilla; water lily

c. Cattail; Bulrush; Sedges; Pondweed

d. Camels; Rats; Snakes; Fish

e. Yak; Mountain goat ; Swan; Sheep

7 Answer the following questions in brief.

a. What type of adaptations do the plants growing in deserts show?

b. What is adaptation? Mention the adaptations of fish to live in aquatic habitat.

c. Explain the adaptations for flight in birds.

d. Explain the adaptations shown by animals living in mountains.

e. Mention the different types of aquatic plants with examples.

8 Answer the following questions in detail.

a. What are the types of aquatic plants? Give one example for each.

b. Explain the adaptations shown by mountain plants.

c. A plant with broad leaves will not survive in a desert. Do you think this statement is correct? Explain.

d. What are the adaptations seen in animals living in deserts to withstand the extreme climatic conditions?

e. Explain the adaptations of plants to air?

9 Think and answer.

a. Suppose you have bought some fish from a store to add to your aquarium at home, what steps would you take to acclimatize the fish to the new environment?

b. What would happen to a mountain plant if the climate changes from very cold to humid and rainy? Can you say what would be the adaptations it would undergo to survive in that?

10 Project

Visit a nearby zoo and make a list of the plants and animals living there. Identify the ones that are not in their natural habitat. Find out how the zoo is helping them adapt to the environment they are living in. Present your report to the class and discuss with your teacher if it is legal to keep animals and plants away from their natural habitat.

11 In the Library

Soil is a habitat for many small creatures such as insects. Soil is rich in humus because of the role of many micro-organisms and other organisms that add nutrients to the soil. Nematodes also play a very important role in the soil. Find out the role of nematodes in the soil and how they are adapted to live in the soil.

Worksheet

Subject Integration

1. **Draw one plant and one animal that are found in any one of the habitats you have studied in the chapter. Discuss their adaptations in class.**

Plant name: ____________	Animal name: ____________
Habitat: ____________	Habitat: ____________

2. **What is your favourite vacation place? Find out and describe its climate, the plants and animals found there and the adaptations they show in order to survive there.**

____

____

____

____

____

____

____

Assessments

Assessment 1 (Chapters 1-5)

Maximum marks: 40

1 Choose the correct answer for each of the following. (5 × 1 = 5)

a. One micron can be mathematically represented as ________.

i. 1/1,000,000 m ii. 1/1000 m iii. 1/10,000,000 m iv. 1/10,000 m

b. Which of these help to speed up metabolic reactions?

i. Fat ii. Carbohydrates iii. Enzymes iv. Proteins

c. Which of these instruments is used to measure blood pressure?

i. Sphygmomanometer ii. Stethoscope iii. Microscope iv. Thermometer

d. Small air sacs present at the end of bronchioles, where the exchange of gases takes place are called

i. lungs ii. bronchi iii. nose iv. alveoli

e. Which of the following plants have tendrils?

i. Citrus plants ii. Cactus iii. Rose plant iv. Pea plant

2 Fill in the blanks. (5 × 1 = 5)

a. Nucleoplasm consists of thread-like structures called ________ (nucleolus/chromosomes).

b. Hydrochloric acid is secreted by ________ (stomach/pancreas).

c. Salivary amylase breaks down ________ (proteins/starch) into maltose.

d. In human beings, breathing in is also called ________ (inhalation/exhalation).

e. Thin, clear lines on the leaf blade of a leaf are called ________ (lamina/veins).

3 Write T for True and F for False. (5 × 1 = 5)

a. Enzymes released by lysosomes digest the cells and its materials.

b. The large intestine mainly absorbs water.

c. Muscle cells in humans can carry out anaerobic respiration.

d. Enzymes released by lysosomes digest the cells and its materials.

e. During photosynthesis carbon dioxide is released from plants.

4 Give reasons for the following. (5 × 2 = 10)

a. Insect-pollinated flowers are brightly coloured.

b. Respiration is different from breathing.

c. Digestion is incomplete without enzymes.

d. Leaves of the Venus flytrap have two lobes.

e. Opuntia plant has leaves modified as spikes.

5 Answer the following questions in brief. **(5 × 3 = 15)**

a. List the cell organelles found exclusively in plant cells and in animal cells and write their importance.

b. Explain the role of different organs of the human digestive system with the help of a labeled diagram.

c. What is double circulation?

d. Explain the mechanism of breathing in human beings.

e. Write a note on leaf modifications in insectivorous plants for trapping insects.

Assessments

Assessment 2 (Chapters 6-7)

Maximum marks: 40

1 Choose the correct answer for each of the following. (5 × 1 = 5)

a. Which of the following is a biodegradable substance?

i. Plastic ii. Paper iii. Glass iv. Metal

b. Which of the following diseases is caused by a virus?

i. Cholera ii. Typhoid iii. Tuberculosis iv. Influenza

c. Which of these is a paired fin in fish?

i. Dorsal fin ii. Caudal fin iii. Anal fin iv. Pelvic fin

d. Which of these is a type of aquatic plants?

i. Terrestrial plants ii. Floating plants

iii. Insectivorous plants iv. Non-green plants

e. Adaptations to a particular surrounding by plants and animals are characterized by their

i. habits and features ii. addiction iii. Both (i) and (ii) iv. None of these

2 Fill in the blanks. (5 × 1 = 5)

a. Secondary sewage treatment involves addition of ____________ (chemicals/microbes) to dissolve suspended particles in water.

b. Typhus fever is a ____________ (vector/water) borne infection.

c. Fish take turns and change directions while swimming with the help of ____________ (paired/unpaired) fins.

d. Pathogen causing malaria is a ____________ (insect/protozoa).

e. The features and habits that enable plants and animals to live and survive in their surroundings are called ____________ (adaptation/habitat).

3 Write T for True and F for False. (5 × 1 = 5)

a. Vitamin C is required for healthy eyes.

b. Vaccination prevents a person from contracting a particular disease.

c. Fish take in water through their mouth and release water through the skin during respiration.

d. Floating plants do not have a stem to fix them to the soil bed.

e. Mountains are habitats found at lower altitudes.

4 Give reasons for the following. (5 × 2 = 10)

a. Taiga has a very harsh environment.

b. Washing and bathing near water bodies should be avoided.

c. Washing hands prevents most of the communicable disease.

d. Underwater plants have thin, ribbon-like leaves.

e. Yaks are sure-footed animals.

5 Answer the following questions in brief. **(5 × 3 = 15)**

a. Explain the adaptations shown by the plants and animals of deserts.

b. What are water-borne diseases? How can they be prevented?

c. What is a habitat? Write a short note on forest habitat.

d. What are the different types of aquatic habitats? Explain any one.

e. What are the measures that can be followed to obtain safe drinking water?